NAT KING COLE

NAT KING COLE

James Haskins
with Kathleen Benson

STEIN AND DAY/*Publishers*/New York

First published in 1984
Copyright © 1984 by James Haskins and Kathleen Benson
All rights reserved, Stein and Day, Incorporated
Designed by Louis A. Ditizio
Printed in the United States of America
STEIN AND DAY/*Publishers*
Scarborough House
Briarcliff Manor, N.Y. 10510

Library of Congress Cataloging in Publication Data

Haskins, James, 1941–
  Nat King Cole.

  Bibliography: p.
  Discography: p.
  Includes index.
  1. Cole, Nat King, 1919–1965.   2. Singers—United
States—Biography.   I. Benson, Kathleen.   II. Title.
  ML420.C63H3   1984   784.5′0092′4   [B]   84-40242
  ISBN 0-8128-2974-3

CONTENTS

Illustrations

Acknowledgments

We are grateful to Irving Ashby, Bumps and Charlie Blackwell, Geri Branton, Carl Carruthers, Benny Carter, Carol Cole, Kelly Cole, Nadine Coles, Joe Comfort, Adeline Hanson, and Nellie Lutcher for sharing their memories of Nat King Cole with us. Thanks also to Halimah Brooks, Ann Kalkhoff and Larry Segal for their help.

Introduction

Nat "King" Cole was only forty-five when he died in 1965, but already he was an institution in the music world. His legendary voice is as familiar today as it was then, yet the passage of twenty years has dimmed the memory of the man. For a person listening to that voice, it is hard to realize that Cole's effortless delivery and words of love masked a profound tension and unhappiness born of frustrations in abundance, over some of which he had control, over many of which he had none.

Twenty years have relegated to ancient history the extreme paradox of being a black star in a racist society, but Nat King Cole lived that paradox. His records sold millions of copies, and women swooned when he sang, but he couldn't be sure of getting a room in a good hotel. They loved him in Vegas, on the stage, but they didn't like his musicians gambling in the casinos or his daughters eating in the dining room. When he performed in the South, he usually had to play before segregated audiences, and when he bowed to Southern customs the National Association for the Advancement of Colored People (NAACP) called him an Uncle Tom. At the same time, fear of Southern opinion kept Madison Avenue advertisers from sponsoring a Nat King Cole television show.

At heart he was a musician, with the potential to be one of the greatest jazz pianists of this century. But his sense of responsibility to his wife and children, as well as his own need for acceptance by a wide audience, caused him to rise from his piano bench to sing, leaving behind a comparatively straightforward but not particularly lucrative career as a jazz instrumentalist for a more commercial and anxiety-provoking life as a pop vocalist. Ironically, his success as a vocalist overshadowed his talent as a pianist to such an extent that even in his own lifetime most people

9

regarded his piano as little more than a prop; that success also prevented him from enjoying the family life that he had sacrificed his instrumental career to build.

Though profoundly saddened by life, Cole never grew embittered. Nor did he ever blame others. He suffered silently and with dignity; and those who knew him felt richer for the experience. For those who did not know him, he left, through his music, a legacy of love that has proved timeless.

NAT KING COLE

1

Prince
of the
Ivories

H E was born on Saint Patrick's Day 1919 and as an adult would enjoy paying homage to that fact by giving his younger children Irish names. But his parents saw nothing special in the coincidence. Or, if they did, they had sense enough to keep it to themselves. In Montgomery, Alabama, in 1919, giving a black child an Irish name would surely have raised eyebrows, and the Reverend Edward James Coles and his wife, Perlina Adams Coles, didn't want to be talked about. The Reverend Mr. Coles was pastor of the First Baptist Church, and they had a position to maintain in their own, black, community in what was then a comparatively small town. Nor did they wish to arouse the suspicions of the white community, some members of which might have suspected that they were trying to put on airs: Niggers had no business giving their children Irish names on Saint Patrick's Day or any other day. The Coleses named their second son Nathaniel Adams Coles.

In complexion and body structure, little Nathaniel was definitely a

Coles, but the strange shape of his eyes must have puzzled his parents. They were wide-set, almost Asiatic, topped by arched brows that gave him a catlike appearance. No one else in the family had those eyes. Southern black folk put great store in distinctive features, and no doubt the elderly in the neighborhood solemnly agreed that the little boy would lead a singular life, though none would have ventured specifics. There was little opportunity in Montgomery for any black to achieve special-ness; it was dangerous to be noteworthy.

Black folks had to be careful in Montgomery, the cradle of the Confederacy. The Civil War was still being fought there. In fact, a lot of white children grew to adulthood steeped in war stories and innocent of the sad fact that the South had lost. Black folks knew the real story, but they kept it to themselves. Better to let the white folks go on thinking whatever they wanted to think; safer that way.

The Reverend Mr. Coles and his wife just wanted to live and let live, raise their family, do the Lord's work. Even such simple goals were difficult for them. The whites acted as if Reconstruction was just yester-day and had to be wiped forcibly from black folks' minds. Forget to keep your head down, to cross over to the other side of the street when one of them approached, look one of them in the eye, and they'd be on you for being uppity, at best—a candidate for lynching, at worst.

Things were better in the North. The U.S.A. was fighting over there in Europe, and a lot of white boys were in the army. Their jobs back home were going begging. Blacks from Montgomery had gone North, gotten jobs, come back home driving big cars and wearing new suits, talking about the North like it was the Promised Land. Edward and Perlina Coles listened and heard and decided to go North, too.

They went to Chicago, probably because they knew people there, people who'd recently moved there from Montgomery and who could help them get started. Chicago was a magnet for blacks from the South. Between 1910 and 1930 almost two hundred thousand of them migrated to that city. And Chicago proved to be a good choice for the Reverend Mr. Coles's family; he found a position as pastor of the Truelight Baptist Church on the South Side of town.

Nathaniel was about four when the family moved to Chicago with his older brother, Edward, Jr., and his sisters Evelyn and Eddie Mae. He was also about four when he first showed musical precocity. He banged out "Yes, We Have No Bananas" on the family piano with both hands. He also liked to stand before the radio and direct the music, using a ruler as a baton. His mother, who served as choir director at all the churches her husband pastored and who also taught music on occasion, encouraged him, as she did all her children. All four of the older children, as well as the two boys who were born much later, Lionel and Isaac, showed considerable musical talent from an early age.

"From the time they were lil' tots, including their sisters, Evelyn and Eddie Mae, they played the church organ and piano, each in his turn, for years in Sunday school and services," the Reverend Mr. Coles once said. "And when there got to be too many pianists in the family, they'd help out singing in the choir." Until he was about twelve, young Nat played by ear. When he reached adolescence, his mother saw to it that he had formal lessons. "I played everything from Bach to Rachmaninoff for years," he told a reporter for the *New York Journal-American* in 1965. At first he didn't want to practice scales and chords. He would listen as his teacher ran over a lesson for him, then simply play it from memory. Finally she convinced him that it was in his best interest to have some technical knowledge of what he was playing; he would be able to become more versatile. Classical music started to have more meaning for him once he began to regard playing it as a challenge to his abilities.

He found that his added technical knowledge helped him when he played in church, trying to translate into notes the exciting musical cadences of his father's sermons. Being composed primarily of recent arrivals from the South, the congregation of the Truelight Baptist Church demanded rousing sermons and music played with feeling. Had young Nat been a rote organ player, he wouldn't have lasted long. The Reverend Mr. Coles took on the pastorate of the Second Progressive Baptist Church, which he later consolidated with Truelight, giving Nat and the other Coles children a still larger audience for their organ playing.

The Coles household was an extremely religious one, of course. Nadine Robinson Coles, Nat's first wife, says that his mother was the stricter parent. "He was . . . regular," she says of the Reverend Mr. Coles. "I could drink a beer with him but not in front of her." But the Reverend Mr. Coles was the physical disciplinarian, enforcing his rules with a collection of straps. Nat liked to recall the time he and Eddie stole the straps and threw them behind an old laundry building: "When Daddy found out, he asked, 'Which one of you did it?' I pointed at Eddie. For a long time after that, I was afraid to go out of the house until I knew where Eddie was."

The Reverend Mr. Coles encouraged his children to have other interests besides music and the church. They were all well-built and well-coordinated, and several of them were excellent athletes. Nat was a talented baseball player and a great baseball fan, and for a youngster with such interests there was no better place to be than Chicago. The newly urbanized black masses embraced Negro league baseball almost as if it were a religion. Donn Rogosin, author of *Invisible Men: Life in Baseball's Negro Leagues,* has observed that baseball was a unifying element for black communities in transition, communities in the process of development. Marching bands, drum majorettes, and parades featuring black dignitaries were as integral to black baseball as parallel festivities were to white baseball. The Chicago American Giants, which became Cole's American Giants in the early 1930s, were followed with all the loyalty and excitement accorded heroes in other areas of life; and no doubt the Coles family felt particularly close to the team once a man named Cole took over its ownership (although they were not related). Chicagoans were especially proud that their city was the site of the annual Negro League East-West Classic. It was, writes Rogosin, "the motive for many middle-class fans to take their summer vacations in Chicago. In fact, the Union Pacific added additional cars on the trains going to Chicago for the East-West Classic."

Chicago was also one of the best places in the world to be if you were interested in jazz, and by the time Nat Coles entered high school he'd become enamored of it. Chicago was alive with that music, and as a major radio center it attracted some of the most talented jazz musicians. Louis Armstrong, Earl "Fatha" Hines, Fletcher Henderson, Jimmie Noone, and a veritable galaxy of others were in residence at the clubs that had sprung up in both the black and white sections of the city during Prohibition and that had become a way of life for Chicagoans by the time the Volstead Act was repealed. Whenever they could, Nat and his older brother, Eddie, went to hear jazz and to listen to the musicians talk. "Our home was near the old Grand Terrace," Nat used to tell interviewers, "and I spent many a night in the alley listening to Earl Hines for ideas." Hines emphasized the right hand in his playing, with strong chords and exciting runs, and he would have a profound effect on Nat's own playing, an influence that Nat always made a point of mentioning. As he told John Tynan of *Down Beat* in 1957, "It was his driving force that appealed to me. . . . He was regarded as the Louis Armstrong of piano players. His was a new, revolutionary kind of playing because he broke away from the eastern style. He broke that barrier, the barrier of what we called 'stride piano,' where the left hand kept up a steady striding pattern."

Hines and his band had opened at the Grand Terrace in December 1928 and began to record for Victor early in 1929. They proved so popular that they became synonymous with the club and were there for years, which was fortunate for young Nat Coles. He could practice Hines's technique at home and, if he didn't think he had his idol's style quite right, go hang out in the alley and listen some more; or ask the King of the Ivories to explain it to him. Another major influence at that time was Jimmie Noone's band; Nat particularly liked Noone's theme song, "Sweet Lorraine." Years later, it was the first song for which he himself became noted.

Naturally, Nat's organ playing began to reflect his outside influences. "My church work was a constant worry to Dad," he once said. "I was inclined to play the accompaniments too much on the hot side, which often resulted in a familiar raising of the eyebrows that meant, 'Tone it down, son, or take the consequences later.'"

As he grew older, Nat found it increasingly difficult to keep jazz influences out of his playing. At Wendell Phillips High School at 39th and Calumet, in the heart of the South Side black community, he found himself in a veritable cradle of jazz. The school produced such jazz notables as Eddie South, Ray Nance, Hayes Alvis, Happy Caldwell, and Milt Hinton in addition to Nat and his older brother, Eddie. And it was not the only high school in Chicago that could boast such illustrious alumni. Across town in the white section, Austin High produced an equivalent number of white jazz artists and is mentioned more often in histories of jazz in Chicago, according to author Stanley Dance in *The World of Earl Hines,* because they were white.

While there was some intermingling of black and white jazz musicians in Chicago, as well as among sporting-life types like gamblers and pimps and prostitutes, the city was, in the main, quite rigidly segregated. While there were no washrooms or drinking fountains marked Colored and White, no laws governing where blacks were to sit on buses, the invisible color bar in Chicago was just as real as the legalized segregation in Montgomery. Living and going to school in the black South Side, Nat Coles was comparatively insulated from direct experiences of white racism. The color prejudice he encountered as a youngster came from members of his own race.

Black Chicagoans, especially the self-styled bourgeoisie, looked down on the poor black migrants from the South; and one of Nat's most vivid childhood memories was of one encounter with this utter disdain. He recalled, "Once, in Chicago, I sat down on a bus next to this light-skinned black lady, and she turned to me and said, 'You are black and you stink and you can never wash it off.'" That experience had a profound effect on young Nathaniel Coles. "That just marked his life," says Geri Branton, who knew Nat for some twenty years. He did not relate the incident to her until about 1956, but it helped her to understand him better. It explained his almost fanatical personal cleanliness. "He was the cleanest person," says Branton, "took two and three baths a day." What else could a kid do after being the object of such a cruel remark? But he had taken that curse inside himself, and no amount of water could ever wash it away.

The Coleses were poor; they were dark-skinned; they spoke in the cadences of the South. While growing up in Chicago was no doubt easier in many ways than growing up in Montgomery would have been, no environment could be friendly to young Nat Coles. That early cruel experience and others like it probably account not only for his extreme personal fastidiousness but also for the shyness and lack of aggressiveness that distinguished him as an adult in a racist society.

By the time he entered high school, Nat Coles was nearly six feet tall. Gangly, though well-coordinated on a baseball field, he was distinguished physically not only by his height but also by his unusual eyes. While his singular appearance may have caused Nat some discomfort while he was growing up, it had its advantages. No one who saw him ever forgot his face, and considering how many young black kids there were who had dreams of musical careers, it didn't hurt to have a face that established musicians would remember and that might help Nat to establish himself as a musician. While at Wendell Phillips High School, both Nat and Eddie, a bass violist, formed their own bands. Nat played in Eddie's for a brief time before organizing his own after Eddie graduated and went East to join Noble Sissle's Society Orchestra, one of the more successful black orchestras of the time. Nat's band was composed of twelve to fourteen pieces and was called Nat Coles and His Rogues of Rhythm, or Royal Dukes—depending on the source. At first they played school and club dances, mostly in exchange for refreshments, and considered themselves lucky if each of them were paid a dollar-fifty a night. Their first break came when another band scheduled to perform at a widely advertised affair at Warwick Hall thought they had the management over a barrel and demanded more money. The Warwick management balked and put out a call for a fill-in band. Nat agreed to play on short notice, and his band was so well received that it began to get more and better dates. One of the biggest thrills of Nat's young career was his victory in a battle of the bands against Hines and his group at the Savoy Ballroom. He was still in high school at the time and fast becoming known as the Prince of the Ivories (Hines, his loss of the battle of the bands at the Savoy notwithstanding, was still the King).

Hines's band at the time included Bud Johnson on tenor sax, Trummy Young on trombone, Omer Simeon on clarinet, Walter Fuller on trumpet, and Wallace Bishop on drums. Hines also had many more arrangements than Nat did, and many of Nat's were copied directly from those of Hines. But the South Side crowd that night at the Savoy pulled for the underdogs, and with the enthusiasm of the audience to spur them on, the young Rogues of Rhythm succeeded in cutting the Hines band to ribbons. At another time, the Rogues took on Ray Nance's local band, but Nat would never say who had won that contest. Whatever its outcome, the performance of the Rogues of Rhythm impressed the management of the Savoy enough to earn them a few jobs playing at dances there.

Hearing of his brother's success, Eddie Coles quit Noble Sissle's Society Orchestra and returned to Chicago, where the brothers teamed up again, this time with a sextet, culling the other four members from the

Rogues of Rhythm: Kenneth Roane on trumpet, Tommy Thompson on alto sax, Bill Wright on tenor sax, and Jimmy Adams on drums. They called the sextet, Eddie Cole's Solid Swingers, dropping the final "s" from their name. As performers, both brothers used the name Cole, although they never took the trouble to make the change legally. The sextet managed to get a six-month booking at the Panama Club on Fifty-eighth Street, which had cradled many other young talents. Bricktop (Ada Smith), queen of the nightclubs in Europe for decades, and singer Florence Mills worked there as members of the Panama Trio in the teens. Nat went to school each weekday morning after having played at the Panama until 2 A.M. He made eighteen dollars a week.

According to Nadine Coles, the elder Coleses never went to the club to see their sons perform; that sort of worldly activity was against their religion. The Reverend Mr. Coles frowned on show business and even regarded it as a competitor of religion, at least where his sons were concerned. "My father objected at first," Nat told a reporter for the *St. Louis Globe-Democrat* in 1955, "especially while I was in school. He had the four sons and he couldn't understand why not one of them would become a minister." The Coles boys had such talent and determination, however, that the Reverend Mr. Coles couldn't bring himself to forbid outright their pursuing careers in music. Even he must have been impressed when the sextet recorded four sides for Decca in July of 1936: "Honey Hush"/"Thunder" and "Bedtime"/"Stomping at the Panama."

To be sure, these were not sides that would ever reach a wide audience. They were "race records," to be sold out of suitcases and off the backs of trucks and in all kinds of ghetto stores. But race records had achieved a modicum of respect in the black community and since the 1920s had been selling five or six million units annually to a black population of about twice that number. In a town like Chicago where musical talent abounded there was intense competition to record; so being recorded was a great coup. Very few of these sides were pressed, and they were collector's items by the mid forties. Nadine Coles has one of these discs.

Nat met Nadine Robinson while he was playing at the Panama Club. She was a dancer there. A native of East St. Louis, Illinois, Nadine had always wanted to be in show business and so had gone to Chicago to pursue her career. "We just started talking," she says, "and one thing led to another." She was about ten years older than Nat. "She was a beautiful woman," says Geri Branton, who met them both in Los Angeles in the 1940s, "magnificent figure." Nat, who called her Shorty, probably was attracted not only to Nadine's beauty but also to her maturity. She had been in show business for a number of years and was willing to advise him about how to further his own career. He took her home to meet his family, and after a while they began to talk about marriage. They "courted about eight months," she says.

On graduating from high school in 1936, Nat could have tried a career in baseball. He reportedly was good enough to have attracted the attention of scouts from two Negro league ball clubs. But playing first base in the always tenuous Negro leagues did not seem to be a very practical choice of career. Young Nat had developed a very methodical way of thinking, and based on his admittedly limited experience, he believed he had a better chance of realizing his dream of being a big band leader like Earl Hines. While baseball would remain a major love of his life, he never regretted choosing music.

After their engagement ended at the Panama Club, Nat and Eddie augmented their group and set out on a Southern tour. It lasted just two weeks. They found themselves stranded in Jackson, Tennessee, without enough money to get back to Chicago. A lot of black groups, and white groups, got stranded in those days. Working on a shoestring, they counted on receipts from each engagement to pay their way to the next, and when a gig was canceled they had no reserves on which to fall back. They managed to talk the driver of their tour bus into accepting their instruments as collateral in return for a ride back to Chicago.

At home again, the brothers and their band and Nadine all got jobs in a revival of *Shuffle Along,* which back in 1920 had been the first all-black show to make it to Broadway and which had ensured the fame of the two entertainer teams who had created it, Sissle and Blake and Miller and Lyles. Eubie Blake, a ragtime pianist and composer, and Noble Sissle, a singer and bandleader, had toured together as The Dixie Duo in an act that was dignified according to the standards of the time (no blackface, which was very unusual in the early years of this century). Flournoy Miller and Aubrey Lyles were a blackface comedy-dancing act. The two teams happened to come together at a National Association for the

Advancement of Colored People (NAACP) benefit in Philadelphia in the summer of 1920 and decided to try to create a show. All agreed that the only way to put black performers onto the white stage with any dignity was through musical comedy. *Shuffle Along* opened in New York at the Sixty-third Street Theater that fall. Several of its songs became classics, among them "I'm Just Wild About Harry" and "In Honeysuckle Time." Its dancing was exuberant. In no time it was a smash hit, and some people date the beginning of the Harlem Renaissance from the time that *Shuffle Along* showed the white folks downtown what exciting things were going on up in Harlem. Well into the 1940s both Sissle and Blake and Miller and Lyles staged revivals of the show. The version that opened in Chicago in 1937 had the backing of Miller and Lyles. Eddie Coles had been with Noble Sissle's orchestra and it's possible that his connection with Sissle enabled the band and Nadine to join the show.

All went well until, after a six-week run in Chicago, the show got set to go on the road. Eddie wanted to remain in Chicago. Nadine wanted to go on tour, and Nat wanted to go with Nadine. Reportedly, the brothers nearly came to blows over the matter. If so, it was one of the few times the even-tempered Nat allowed himself to display so much emotion. In the end, Nat and Nadine and most of the band went with the show. Eddie and several of the original sextet stayed in Chicago. The two brothers didn't speak to each other for months.

"We were married on the road, in Ipsalante, Michigan," says Nadine, who now lives in St. Louis and acknowledges that people pass over her name in the telephone book because they are looking for Nadine Cole. Her married name was Coles and she has kept it. "Actually," she says, "we were married twice. We'd made arrangements to get married at the home of some people we were going to be staying with. But we decided not to wait. We were married by a judge in Ipsalante, and then two days later, in the next town, we got married as planned."

They reached Long Beach, California, two months after leaving Chicago. There, a member of the troupe ran off with eight hundred dollars in receipts. The group needed that money to keep going, and without it the show folded. The newlyweds found themselves stranded on the West Coast. Nat wanted to return to Chicago, but he was too proud to ask his family for help. Nadine wanted them to stay in California and try their luck there. Apparently, she was more sure of her husband's ability to succeed than he was. "Nadine is Nat's first real fan," wrote Alyce Key in a newspaper column called Keynotes around 1943. "She always believed in him and has a strong influence with him. It was upon her insistence that he remained in California and it was Nadine's faith and loyalty along with the help of an auntie of Nadine's with whom they lived that encouraged the young pianist who was realizing the bitter struggle that so often goes with the building of a career."

Most of the members of the band stayed, too, and Nat managed to get a few bookings at dances and social club affairs. According to Nellie Lutcher, his brother Eddie later joined him. Lutcher, a native of Lake Charles, Louisiana, was a singer who eventually recorded with Nat. She and her husband and child were living in Los Angeles a block away from Central Avenue. "My son was just an infant, so it was around 1937," says Lutcher. "We shared a house with Lloyd Wilson, a musician friend, and his wife. Lloyd knew a lot of musicians, and when anybody new came to town he would meet them and bring them home. They would have jam sessions at the house. I met Nat when Lloyd brought him home and asked if it would be okay if he rehearsed at the house. I said, sure it would be all right. So they came over and rehearsed with this big band. I met his wife, Nadine. She was a nice person. I met his brother Eddie, who played bass and piano."

The band rehearsed frequently and performed whenever they could get bookings. Fairly often they traveled to other West Coast cities. Nadine accompanied the band as a dancer and recalls that period as a pleasant one. She and Nat would take long walks, exploring each city. "We would sing songs and write songs together," she says. "We were together all the time."

Nat wanted very much to have children, and they tried; but Nadine miscarried two or three times over the years. Her inability to have children was a source of disappointment for Nat, but they had much else to share. They were poor but happy together doing what they loved.

Jazz lyricist and manager Charlie Carpenter told Stanley Dance that back in those early days Nat not only was poor, he looked poor. "But although Nat didn't have any money, Nadine would wash and starch his shirts, press his clothes and everything, and then he would come out sharp as a tack." Nat always looked neat and professional when applying for a job—like he didn't need the job to buy the next week's groceries.

According to Nadine, Nat was not particularly ambitious. "He never talked about being a star someday." He simply wanted to make a living playing his music, leading his band. Unfortunately, even that simple ambition was difficult to realize in Los Angeles. Musically it was not a swinging town, and its relatively small black population could not support many dances or other large affairs requiring a band. The white population hired white bands for their large affairs. There wasn't much interest in blacks as entertainers and certainly not in other areas of life. Hollywood was a racist town, as blacks who migrated there soon learned. A few years later Lena Horne suffered considerable discrimination when she and her children moved there; and Lena Horne was light-skinned. Eventually Nat was forced to give up his band.

With a seven-piece combo he got a job at the Ubangi Club in Maywood for a while, but after that he couldn't seem to find any more bookings. He had to put aside his dream of being leader of a musical group of any size and take whatever work he could get as a solo piano player. "I played every beer joint from San Diego to Bakersfield," he used to say.

Many of these gigs were one-night stands, and in addition to being hard on the man they were hard on the musician. While Nat didn't have to tote his instrument around with him and so was more mobile than, say, a bass player like Eddie, he never knew what kind of instrument awaited him. Most beer joints didn't sport Steinways, needless to say. More often than not he found an old upright, badly out of tune. Club owners didn't want to hear that their piano was at fault, they wanted to hear good music. Nat had to struggle with the instruments, and he didn't always win. On occasion, he had to voice all his chords differently, to avoid an obstreperous note, but received no more money for his trouble. Nor were beer joint patrons the ideal audience for a serious musician. Nat much preferred studio work and took whatever jobs he could find.

Bumps Blackwell, who had a struggling band of his own called Bumps Blackwell's Junior Band, recalls meeting Nat around that time. "He was rehearsal pianist for Flournoy Miller's show *Running Wild.* He was also a studio pianist, playing behind a guy named Frankovich. That name didn't look good on the label copy so they changed the guy's name to Frankie Laine. Frankie Laine's first big recording, 'To Spend the Night with You,' has Nat on the piano." Blackwell has served as mentor for a variety of talented musicians and singers in the course of his career: "I'm the one who started Sam Cooke and Lou Rawls. In Seattle, I started Ray Charles, Quincy Jones." He recognized the talent in the young pianist from Chicago, but at the time he wasn't in a position to help him.

It was a difficult period for Nat. He wasn't making any money to speak of, and at times he longed to be at home, where at least people knew him and appreciated his music. Forced to go wherever someone would pay him, he was away from Nadine more than he wanted to be, and when he was with her he felt guilty about not being able to provide for her. At such times his dignity suffered. At one point he was so desperate for money that he rummaged through the few songs he had written and made the rounds of music publishers on Vine Street, Hollywood's Tin Pan Alley. He later recalled, "At the end of the afternoon, footsore and weary, I sold 'Straighten Up and Fly Right' to a publisher for fifty dollars—outright, no royalties."

The title of the song was that of a sermon he'd often heard his father deliver in church; the lyrics told the story of a buzzard who takes a little monkey on a skyride. The man who bought Nat's original composition was Irving Mills, a man who knew his music. An impressario par excellence who managed both Duke Ellington and Cab Calloway during his career, he had been a successful song publisher since the 1920s. He had an ear for a tune that would sell and the savvy to pay as little as he could for it. Young Nat was in no position to bargain; in fact, he was grateful for the money he did get. It tided him over until the next gig.

In the fall of 1937, Nat was hired at the Century Club (formerly the Trouville) on Santa Monica Boulevard in Los Angeles. It was a favorite hangout for musicians, and it was there that he began to develop a small following among his peers. "All the musicians dug him," says Bumps Blackwell. "We went there just to listen to him because nobody was like him. That cat could play! He was unique."

In the course of playing on all those out-of-tune uprights, Nat had created his own style. Though the influence of Earl Hines was immediately discernible, in Nat's playing neither hand was dominant. Such balance suited his temperament.

Bob Lewis, manager of the Swanee Inn on North La Brea, also started coming to hear him. At length he told Nat that he was interested in trying out a quartet in his club. If Nat could get a quartet together, he'd pay them each twenty-five dollars a week. For Nat, who had never made more than five dollars a night as a solo on the West Coast, this was an offer he couldn't refuse, even though he had never seriously considered heading a small combo. He wasted no time rounding up a guitarist, a bass violist, and a drummer.

Oscar Moore was the guitarist. A native of Austin, Texas, who had come to the West Coast with his family from Phoenix, Arizona, about a year before Nat had arrived, he already enjoyed a good reputation in Hollywood and often worked for the movie studios. He was the same age as Nat. Twenty years later, he told John Tynan of *Down Beat* about the first time he met Nat. It was around 1936 at the Paradise Café on Main Street in Los Angeles. Oscar had gone there to hear Lionel Hampton's group. So had Nat. "First time I laid eyes on Nat, he looked like a real mean guy—his eyes almost closed, glintin' out at you, diggin' what was goin' on. After I met him, I found out how wrong I was."

Coincidentally, Wesley Prince was also at the Paradise Cafe that night, for at the time he was working with Hampton. The round-faced Prince became the bassist for Nat's group. Had Eddie Coles been around then, Nat surely would have asked him to join the quartet. But Eddie had gone back East. He remained there, leading various groups. In the early 1940s he had a trio called "Three Loose Nuts" that did a musical comedy act. In 1949–50 he and a group recorded six sides for the Gotham label in Philadelphia. In the absence of Eddie, Nat chose Wesley Prince. A native of Pasadena, Prince was, like Nat, the son of a Baptist minister; he was a few years older than Nat and Oscar.

Lee Young, drummer, agreed to complete the quartet, but he was unenthusiastic about it. He really wanted to play with a big band. On opening night at the Swanee Inn, he failed to show, rendering the quartet a trio. Manager Bob Lewis, however, was happy enough with the group's sound not to quibble.

Most sources and Cole legend credit Bob Lewis with giving Nat the nickname he would carry for the rest of his life. "Coles, huh," he is supposed to have mused, "Old King Cole. . . ." On opening night, Nat told Sharon A. Pease of *Down Beat,* Lewis said, "If we are going to book you as 'King' Cole, you will have to look the part," and produced a gold leaf crown. Though eager to please his new boss, Nat didn't like playing the clown. "I wore the crown for about three weeks," he told Pease; "then one night it mysteriously disappeared. It worked out as I had hoped—he never got around to getting another one." Henceforth, Nat was Nat King Cole. His trio was called the King Cole Swingsters. Originally they were engaged at the Swanee Inn for a month. They wound up staying six months, in the course of that time developing a memorable sound that was marked by an almost perfect blending of their instruments so that it was difficult for the untrained ear to distinguish who was responsible for what and for the trained ear not to be enraptured.

2

The King
Cole Trio

L EGEND has it that none of the trio considered singing until a drunken customer at the Swanee Inn demanded that Nat sing "Sweet Lorraine" one night. According to Maria Cole, that legend became so firmly entrenched in the public's mind that Nat gave up trying to set things straight. Besides, it was a good story. A drunk did demand that Cole sing "Sweet Lorraine" Jimmie Noone's theme song back in Nat's Chicago days, and other songs one night while the trio was playing at the Swanee Inn; but it was not the first time Nat or the others had sung for the club's customers. In her biography of her husband, Maria, Nat's second wife, quotes a radio interview in which Nat said, "When I organized the King Cole Trio back in 1937, we were strictly what you would call an instrumental group. To break the monotony, I would sing a few songs here and there between the playing. I sang things I had known over the years. I wasn't trying to give it any special treatment,

29

just singing. I noticed thereafter people started requesting more singing, and it was just one of those things."

The story also goes that in its early years the group that came to be called the King Cole Trio (some sources credit Wesley Prince for giving it that name) had to struggle for acceptance. There is considerable truth to that part of the legend. Big bands, not small combos, were the rage. In fact, trios were practically unheard of. According to Cole, agents used to refer to the group as the "Chamber Music Boys." Nat once told Ralph J. Gleason of the *San Francisco Chronicle,* "I'd go up to the booking offices and see the big men, and they'd say, 'You've got an awkward combination there, boy.' But I never believed them. I knew they were just saying that to get rid of me, and I knew they didn't know what they were talking about." At times, however, he became discouraged. He hadn't been able to make it with a big band, or even a seven-piece combo. Now, with a trio, he was told he had an "awkward combination." J. T. Gipson, who worked briefly as the trio's press agent, recalled a time when he saw Cole in front of the Club Alabam in the wee hours of a rainy night and, recognizing him, told him to get in out of the rain. Dejectedly, Cole replied, "I ain't got sense enough to."

To be sure, Cole and his group were not making big money, nor were they getting the recognition he felt they should have. But they suffered through only a couple of lean, virtually anonymous years, 1937 to 1938. After that, they enjoyed fairly steady work, though they still didn't make much money. After leaving the Swanee Inn, the trio worked at Jim Otto's Steak House, Foxhill's Café opposite the Twentieth Century-Fox lot, Shep Kelley's in Hollywood, the Club Circle in Beverly Hills. In several of these clubs they were the first blacks to perform. "We were the first group of any kind to break in cocktail lounges out there," Nat said around 1943. "Hollywood never had been the place for them. But Bob Lewis took a chance—gave us our chance—and the breaks were right and we did all right."

Lionel Hampton asked them to record with him on Victor in 1939. "Central Avenue Breakdown," "Jack the Bellboy," "A Ghost of a Chance," "Dough Re Me," "Blue Because of You," "Jivin' With Jarvis," "House of Morgan," and "I'd Be Lost Without You" were Hampton's biggest selling records that year and caused him to announce that the trio would be incorporated into his new band that fall. At least that's what Leonard Feather reported in *Down Beat.* Nothing came of the idea; Cole and his two sidemen preferred to remain a small combo.

The trio made their first recordings as a group between 1938 and 1939 for Davis & Schwegler: "Riffin' at the Bar–B–Q," "I Lost Control of Myself" (vocal by Bonnie Lake), "Let's Get Happy," and "That Please Be Mineable Feeling." They had a sustaining series on NBC radio in 1938, and the show contributed to their increasing popularity among the small but enthusiastic group of jazz aficionados in Los Angeles and environs. At the Radio Room, a bowling alley across Vine Street from NBC, they were performers in residence for fourteen months and "made a lot of friends," as Nat put it.

In the meantime, the members of the trio became friends, going out together with their wives, talking about baseball, getting to know each other's moods. "Oscar knows what I'm going to do before I do," Nat was fond of saying. Their music reflected their warm personal relationship. All contributed to the trio's sound, not just riffs and chords, but voices. When they injected a little singing it was often of the ensemble variety. Moore and Prince also wrote lyrics. In late 1940 they recorded four sides for Decca's Sepia Series: "Sweet Lorraine," "This Side Up," "Honeysuckle Rose," and "Gone with the Draft," the last a comical tune written by Wesley Prince and the first on that subject.

Early the next year, Cole recorded independently of his two sidemen, experimenting with a quartet. A King Cole Quartet with Cole on piano and vocals, Lee Young on drums (the same Lee Young whom Cole had lined up for his quartet at the Swanee Inn back in 1937), and unknown musicians on guitar and bass recorded for the combined labels of Varsity, Savoy, and Ammor. According to Leon René, interviewed by Arnold Shaw for the book *Honkers and Shouters,* the primary label was Ammor, though in Shaw's book the name is Amour:

"Jack Gutshall, a jukebox operator, asked me to A & R [find Artists and Repertory] his new label called Amour Records. He needed new R & B [Rhythm and Blues] artists for his jukeboxes, so I started scouting for new talent. I recorded Nat at the old Melrose Studio (used by Decca). In those days, they were still cutting masters on wax cylinders (unused masters were scrapped and used again). When the session was completed,

I played the masters for Jack: 'Black Spider,' 'River Street Marie' [Sainte Marie, actually], 'I Like to Riff,' and 'Sunny Side of the Street.' He liked the 'hot' numbers but turned down 'Sweet Lorraine,' which became one of Nat's biggest hits."

Also in early 1941, Cole, Moore, and Prince went on their first tour. Arranged by Tom Rockwell of the General Amusement booking agency, who had approached them soon after they had recorded for Decca, the tour was not a series of one-nighters but several months of extended engagements, the minimum being four weeks.

In Chicago they filled in for the Bob Crosby band at the Panther Room of the Hotel Sherman. They also played at the Blue Note. Although Cole liked to joke that "No one knew we were there except our families," he was proud to return to that city with his own group.

Traveling in a beat up, second-hand car and lacking proper clothes for performing, The King Cole Trio played at the Rendezvous in Philadelphia, the Hotel Senator and the Romany in Washington, D.C., and then fulfilled every musician's dream by playing the Big Apple—four weeks at Nick's in Greenwich Village and then eight months, off and on, at Kelly's Stable on West Fifty-second Street.

According to Arnold Shaw, who wrote *The Rockin' '50s,* Cole's debut as a singer occurred while the trio was playing Kelly's Stable:

"One afternoon, co-owner Ralph Watkins received a phone call from his sister, who was the Stable's bookkeeper. She couldn't do her work because Nat was 'singin' this one number over and over until I'm goin' nuts.' Watkins said, 'Nat doesn't sing,' and hopped into a cab and sped over to the club. Making a quiet entrance, he parked himself in a corner of the darkened club and listened—in surprise. He said nothing to Nat until a few nights later when Billie Holiday, the starring vocalist on the bill, called in sick. Then he tackled Cole about taking the vocal spot for the evening. Cole balked, exhibiting an uneasiness that surprised Watkins. But that evening, he sang. It was the first time that King Cole, jazz pianist, appeared as Nat Cole, singer."

While Shaw is incorrect about when Cole first sang in public, his anecdote reveals that at the time Cole's talent as a singer was practically unknown.

The trio hardly took New York City by storm. Nor did they make a lot of money. At Nick's the scale was thirty dollars a week and forty-five dollars for a leader; legend has it that Nat couldn't even get a thirty dollar advance to make a payment on his car. At Kelly's Stable, they got one hundred forty a week, total, but they gained invaluable experience.

Kelly's Stable had moved to 52nd Street early in 1940 and taken over a spot that had been known briefly as O'Leary's Barn, after the famous structure that started the big Chicago Fire. There was sawdust on the floor, carriage lamps at each side of the small stage; musicians worked in front of a large mural depicting a trotter on a race track. The trio got into Kelly's Stable because Ralph Watkins had heard the sixteen bars by an unknown trio on the Lionel Hampton recording of "Jack the Bellboy" and made it his business to find them. Cole and his sidemen were forever grateful, for while at Kelly's they were immersed in the jazz of the "street that never slept."

Prior to 1939, the club, which was on the more westerly and less important block of Swing Street (near Seventh Avenue), had been overshadowed by the Onyx and the Famous Door. But in 1939 Billie Holiday began to build a following there. In the same year, Coleman Hawkins also started to attract a large audience there. Thus, by the time Nat and Oscar and Wesley arrived, the Stable was no slouch as a jazz forum. At one point, they shared a bill with Benny Carter and his sextet, Art Tatum working as a solo, and a blues shouter named Ma Rainey. Another time they accompanied Billy Daniels. When they weren't playing at Kelly's, they were free to drop in on jam sessions elsewhere on the street. At Hickory House across the street, on any given night, Count Basie, Teddy Wilson, Hot Lips Page, Chu Berry, Roy Eldridge, the Dorseys, Artie Shaw, or Benny Goodman might drop in. Frank Sinatra and Frankie Laine might be hanging around, waiting for a chance to sing. On Sundays there were jam sessions at Jimmy Ryan's where Cole and his sidemen could improvise with Fats Waller, Earl Hines, and Eddie Heywood.

It may have been during that stay in New York that Cole recorded four sides for V-Disc with a Quintet that included Shad Collins on trumpet, Illinois Jacquet on tenor sax, Gene Englund on bass, and J. C. Heard on drums. There was a lot of experimenting in sound going on, which made the New York part of the tour a largely positive experience for Cole.

33

The tour, even though it was not a series of one-nighters, was difficult for the trio. In strange cities they had to be constantly on their guard, lest they inadvertently stray into a white neighborhood. While the cities where they played had little legalized segregation, there was plenty of the informal variety. Even middle-class blacks were likely to shun the members of the trio if they did not know who they were, for most show people were poorly regarded by the black bourgeoisie. But the trio did have steady work during the tour, and they gained more recognition in the music world. In the fall of 1941, *Down Beat* ran its first column on Cole. "Nat plays all styles well," wrote columnist Sharon A. Pease, "slow blues, boogie, and jump tunes. He does an exceptionally fine job on slow evergreens—when you catch the gang, request 'I Can't Get Started,' for a good example."

Around March 1942 the trio returned to Los Angeles and went into the 331 Club for eight months, supplementing their incomes with whatever other jobs they could find. Norman Granz provided one such outside source of income—six dollars a night jamming at Billy Berg's.

Born in Los Angeles, Granz had worked his way through the University of California at Los Angeles by clerking at a brokerage house. While at UCLA he'd acquired the hobby of collecting phonograph records, and his burgeoning interest in jazz had led him to Nat Cole by 1941. Granz was keen to know more about jazz, and Cole obliged. Soon, Granz was visiting Cole regularly, bringing stacks of jazz records for listening, then having dinner with Nat and Nadine. Granz then decided to arrange jam sessions featuring the best jazz musicians in town.

A new musicians union rule guaranteeing regularly employed musicians one night off weekly provided the personnel. What made the idea particularly attractive to jazz musicians was that tables were put on Billy Berg's dance floor—these jam sessions were for serious listening. Black musicians were attracted by another Granz innovation: The Hollywood night clubs had a fixed rule against admitting black patrons, but at Granz's jam sessions they were to be admitted.

The jam sessions began in 1942 and were an immediate success. Duke Ellington's and Jimmie Lunceford's bands performed at them when they were in town. Lester Young and his brother Lee were regulars, as was Nat Cole, whom Granz referred to as his house pianist.

The trio also backed up the Dandridge sisters in the early 1940s. The young women, who were really two sisters, Dorothy and Vivian, and a nonsister, Etta, were billed as sepia Andrews Sisters and had achieved some fame at the Cotton Club in New York in the late 1930s. Dorothy would later star in films. She married Harold Nicholas, one of the famous dance team, the Nicholas Brothers, and that is how Geri Branton came to meet Nat and Nadine. Geri was then married to the other Nicholas brother, Fayard. She remembers how impressed she was with the sound of the King Cole Trio. "It was unreal what they were doing—matching each other note for note in the *same* tempo. It was unbelievable."

World War II interfered briefly with that sound. In August 1942 Wesley Prince, who had written "Gone with the Draft," was drafted. Red Callender replaced him for a short time as bassist before Johnny Miller took permanent possession of the spot. A native of Pasadena like Prince, Miller had played with a number of big bands, among them that of C. P. Johnson. He had a driving style that provided the group with a secure rhythmic base, and Nat was fairly sure that the trio could go on as before. He was also quite certain that there would be no more changes in personnel necessitated by the war. He himself had been classified 4F; as reported in the press at the time, the reason was "nervous hypertension," although in her book Maria said the reason was flat feet. Oscar Moore and Johnny Miller were both family men and did not expect to be called unless there was a general call for fathers.

It is said that Oscar Moore was having some family problems in 1942; he also had some problems with his health. He missed several outside gigs of the trio's, including Norman Granz's jam sessions. Two times in a row Moore failed to show up, forcing Cole and Miller to play duets. Moore's lack of dependability at that time may be one reason why Cole recorded several pieces with two other sidemen in New York in July 1942. On the other hand, since the recordings were arranged by Norman Granz, perhaps Granz simply chose the personnel he wished to record. All on Philo & Aladdin Album I (a 12″ disc), the numbers were "Indiana," "I Can't Get Started," "Tea for Two," and "Body and Soul." Cole's two sidemen were Red Callender on bass and Lester Young (Lee Young's brother and a member of Count Basie's band) on tenor sax.

While Cole did do some recording with others besides Moore and

Miller, there was no question that they were his two "main men." They appeared in several feature-length films in 1943 and 1944, including *Calling All Stars* for Columbia and two for Republic/USA (*Here Comes Elmer* and *Pistol Packin' Mama*). These were minor films, and the trio's scenes the easily cuttable kind that Southern exhibitors demanded of the film studios (Southern censors cut every segment that featured blacks in roles other than servants or jungle natives). There was nothing notable about these films except, perhaps, *Pistol Packin' Mama,* about which one columnist wrote, "For what is believed to be the first time in Hollywood history, a Negro musicombo draws dignified, sensible presentation in Republic's *Pistol Packin' Mama,* in which King Cole Trio appears and plays straight without Hollywood hokum." They also appeared in two 3-minute "shorties" for U.S.A., backing up vocalist Ida James in *Is you or isn't you my baby?* and featured in *I'm a shy guy.*

Also, except for two sides on which Red Callender played bass, Moore and Miller played on all the recordings Cole made in 1943. The two were "All for You" and "Vom Vim Veedle" on the Excelsior label.

Excelsior was a small black recording firm in Los Angeles founded by Otis René, a songwriter and brother of Leon René, that recorded the trio on six sides that year. The other four were "I'm Lost" by Otis René, "Pitchin' Up a Boogie," "Beautiful Moons Ago," and "Let's Spring One." Not many of the records were pressed, and by the time the Cole Trio hit big they were collector's items. A couple of reviews are in the Cole papers at the University of Southern California (USC).

"All for You"/"Vom Vim Veedle" (by Bob Scherman) was difficult to obtain even when first issued, but one reviewer, who called the trio "probably the finest jazz unit of its type," wrote that it was worth seeking out. "Cole's singing and talented pianisms, coupled with the guitar work of Oscar Moore, make 'All' a delightful performance. The reverse . . . is a bright nonsense item."

Of "Pitchin' Up a Boogie"/"I'm Lost," another reviewer wrote, "For all we know this disc may be obtainable only in the San Fernando Valley. We got an odd copy from the coast and we're going to review it anyway. It seems to hail from the same date as that wonderful 'All for You.' 'Boogie' has a puerile lyric, but don't worry, there's no boggie-woogie— just some of Cole's finest Hines-style piano, Oscar Moore's moving, grooving guitar, and the two of them riffing together excitingly. 'Lost' is a fine ballad by Otis René, sung in the royal Cole manner with only eight bars off for piano. One of the big companies should buy this up."

On November 1, 1943, the trio recorded for another small company, Premier, "My Lips Remember Your Kisses," "F.S.T.," "Let's Pretend," and "Got a Penny" (not issued). But in this case, too, few records were pressed. Not only were the companies too small to finance a large issue of a record, but also they had to contend with materials shortages. The early years of U.S. participation in the war were difficult for record companies, as they were for other enterprises not crucial to the war effort. Shortages of building materials brought most new construction to a halt. Shortages of shellac drastically reduced the production of new records. Even big companies like Victor suffered, and small, black-owned companies like Excelsior and Premier barely managed to stay alive.

Leon René told Arnold Shaw how he and his brother Otis established their own record-pressing plant and kept it going: "The press needed stock, so we went hunting all over town for discarded records at stores that had old disks that they wanted to get rid of. We paid them one cent each. In those days there were few R & B-record stores. R & B records were sold in furniture stores, drug stores, makeshift store fronts, shoeshine stands—anywhere—to meet the demand for R & B records.

"As sales increased, so did the demand for old records. We went to two cents per record until the supply was exhausted. All the old records were brought to our one-press plant in Culver City where we reheated them on a steam table. The centers were cut out and the stock rolled into a ball and put into the press where the finished record was completed. Since we used old records of different colors, the finished record looked like a rainbow, but it didn't matter if you had a hit."

Cole and the others knew that records were the key to the big time. As Ted Fox notes in his book *Showtime at the Apollo,* records were becoming major consumer items: "During the 1930s only twenty-six records each sold a million copies or more. Between 1940 and 1945 the figure rose to sixty-eight, and between 1945 and 1950 there were eighty-two. At first, the record companies complained that 75 percent of their output was going to jukeboxes, but as home record players became increasingly popular consumers began buying discs themselves." Thus, the King Cole

Trio recorded whenever possible and for whatever label would have them, hoping for a hit in the only market that was open to them—the Negro, or race, market.

Music, and records, were as segregated in those days as was the society in which they flourished. Black records were confined to the small rhythm and blues field. According to Arnold Shaw in *The Rockin' '50s,* "In Manhattan you had to go to One Hundred Twenty-fifth Street if you wanted to buy a best-selling R & B platter.... And to hear them on radio, you had to go searching for the small-wattage stations at the top of the dial." In the L.A. area, the stores selling black records were all in Watts, the black ghetto. Black singers had little hope of being recorded on a major label, unless it was for its sepia series. Nor did they have much chance of reaching the wider, white, audience. A few black female singers had managed this crossover, among them Billie Holiday, Ethel Waters, and Ella Fitzgerald. But in general, even the most exciting black singer had no chance of reaching the white audience, while less distinctive white singers achieved considerable fame.

Still, with the record and jukebox business flourishing, the race market was a growing and potentially lucrative one. Cole and his musicians wanted to be a part of it.

Important, too, was publicity. The trio wasn't making enough money to be able to afford big-time managers and publicists, but by early 1943 Cole had decided they should try to get at least some small-time people to work for them. In 1948, J. T. Gipson, columnist for the *California Eagle,* recalled how he became Cole's first press secretary:

"My business relationship with the King started one afternoon back in 1943 when his Royal Highness came by my office to offer me a job as press agent for the trio. They were then working for two hundred and fifty dollars a week, entertaining at a classy Los Angeles saloon called the 331 Club. Confidentially, I was working for much less, slaving at the *California Eagle.* So I accepted the job, in addition to my other duties on the West's oldest weekly. We (meaning Nat and I) got along fine up to the week I forgot to put a picture of the trio in the paper. That made Cole hot! He thought it was a %C..**'y shame that such an important picture didn't get in the paper. The 'important' picture was a shot taken at the swank Trocadero night club in Hollywood with Walter Winchell. The pose showed Winchell being serenaded by the trio. It was a publicity shot (for the King) and the picture appeared in *Downbeat* and nearly every other trade magazine and paper (but mine!) in the country. Reason for its omission being that I had difficulty deciding between the Winchell-King pic or one of beauteous Betty Grable in a flesh-colored bathing suit to decorate my theatrical page. Needless to state the Grable pic won out. Needless to state, I was fired from further writing duties with the King Cole trio. I never held that against the boys. . . ."

Cole had better luck with his choice of a personal manager. He and his sidemen were playing at the 331 Club when he called Carlos Gastel and asked him to drop by. The two had met when the trio had played at the Foxhills Café in the late 1930s. Gastel, a native of Honduras who had moved to California with his family while still a child, was at that time a recent graduate of the University of California at Los Angeles (UCLA) and determined to make a career as an entertainment manager. Among his first clients were orchestras headed by young men named Sonny Dunham and Stan Kenton. Neither group was having much success, and Gastel was leery of taking on additional clients who couldn't pay him. According to Maria Cole, Nat had asked him earlier to represent the trio and Gastel had turned him down. This time, Cole wanted to ask Gastel to suggest a manager, and as Maria tells it Gastel surprised even himself by offering to take the job.

Gastel had discovered jazz while at UCLA and had been an early fan of the trio. He had followed their career, taken note of their increased recording activity, their films, their tour in 1941 to 1942, and decided that they could become much more successful if managed correctly. He was now willing to throw in his lot with them. He and Cole drew up papers formalizing their relationship. According to Maria, Cole wanted to begin paying Gastel a small salary immediately, but Gastel said he would not take a percentage until the group was earning eight hundred dollars a week. Three weeks later he asked for and got that salary for the group at the Orpheum theater in Los Angeles, an auspicious start for a relationship that was to last twenty years and be one of the closest and most lucrative in the history of the entertainment business.

After completing their engagement at the Orpheum, the trio played ten weeks at the Beachcombers' Club in Omaha, Nebraska, then returned to the 331 Club for forty-eight weeks. The club's owner, Herb Rose, spoke more than once during that time of keeping the group there "for the duration." That was fine with Nat: "No more roamin'," he said. "That Ain't Right," which the trio had recorded for Decca, began to hit the "colored jukeboxes" while they were at the 331 Club and eventually made number one on the Harlem Hit Parade. Perhaps that's why Glen Wallichs approached Nat that fall with the idea of recording for Capitol Records.

Capitol, founded in 1942, was another small company, but it had a greater chance for growth than most new companies begun at that time. Its founders knew the business and had fairly substantial capital. Glen Wallichs, one of the three partners, owned a record store in Los Angeles called Music City. Cole had played at its opening in 1940, and Wallichs had been following him ever since. The second partner was songwriter Johnny Mercer, who had an ear for what would sell and numerous contacts in the business. The third was movie producer Buddy DeSylva. He had the money and put up some twenty-five thousand dollars to get Capitol on its feet. The first two acts the company signed were Freddie Slack with Ella Mae Morse and Jo Stafford and the Pied Pipers.

Capitol got around the problem of wartime shellac shortages by buying up old discs and grinding them up to recycle them into new records. But hardly had they started to do so when they were confronted with another problem: On August 1, 1942, James C. Petrillo, head of the American Federation of Musicians, had called a strike and forbade all members of the union from making new records. While the ban did not affect vocalists directly, it forced them to sing a cappella; and most vocalists did not want to record without instrumental backgrounds. Most record companies didn't want to record a cappella vocals, and most record buyers didn't want to buy them. The record companies tried a variety of measures to get around the ban. Some had instrumental backgrounds recorded in England, but a company had to have big money to do that. Most companies, including Capitol, tried to find master recordings, pressed before the ban, to buy and reissue. Wallichs believed that some of the recordings the King Cole Trio had done were worth reissuing.

Capitol bought the master of "All for You"/"Vom Vim Veedle" from Excelsior and issued it on October 15, 1943; it immediately got better play than the Excelsior disc. Two weeks later, Petrillo lifted his ban on new recordings, and Cole and Capitol were free to work on fresh material. On November 30, Cole, Moore, and Miller went into the Capitol studios and recorded four sides: "Straighten Up and Fly Right," "Gee, Ain't I Good to You," "Jumpin' at Capitol," and "If You Can't Smile and Say Yes, Please Don't Cry and Say No." Two weeks later they recorded four more: "Sweet Lorraine," "Embraceable You," "It's Only a Paper Moon," and "I Can't See For Lookin.'"

"Straighten Up and Fly Right," Cole's own composition and the song he had sold outright for fifty dollars back in 1937, was a major hit in the Negro market and among white jazz fans. It was unique in that it appealed to both jazz lovers and the less particular general public. Cole's piano playing was extraordinary—smooth, fantastic voicing and chords. On the other hand, it was a novelty tune, and in the war years the public seemed to need novelty. By May 1944 the record had become one of the biggest hits of the year, climbing from eighth place to third place on the charts in just one week. It sold over a million copies. Irving Mills netted twenty-five thousand dollars in royalties; Cole didn't get a cent. When the record began to sell well, Cole filed suit against Mills, claiming that Mills held only the right to publish the song, not to collect royalties from a recording of it with which he'd had nothing to do. But Mills had a contract showing that Cole had sold him the song outright, and Cole lost his suit. It was a bitter experience for him. Not for several years was he able to look back philosophically and say, "I've done better since." Still, the record brought the King Cole Trio its first national fame, and with Ella Mae Morse's "Cow Cow Boogie" put the fledgling Capitol Records on its feet. Nat would remain with Capitol Records for the rest of his life, apparently cheating only for his friend Norman Granz. In 1944 Granz started to present monthly jazz concerts at the Philharmonic, concerts he subsequently recorded in the popular Jazz at the Philharmonic series. Pianists on some of those recordings who are identified as "A Guy" and "Shorty Nadine" were both really Nat King Cole.

As 1944 began, the King Cole Trio were playing until midnight at the 331 Club, then going over to a new after-hours club, the Last Word, on Central Avenue. In both places they drew ever larger audiences, including a number of musicians who had decided that if the Cole Trio could be successful, then other small combos could be, too. Wrote Barry Ulanov, the editor of *Metronome,* in 1944, "Man for man, this is *the* great trio, *the* great small unit, and I'm not excepting the Art Tatum Trio, for while Tatum himself is without compeer, his associates don't match Nat's. Art has said many times, too, how much he'd like to have Oscar on guitar. He has admitted, too, that it's the King Cole Trio which inspired the formation of the Tatum ditto. He was a constant listener to Cole sessions when he was on the coast in '43." Within a few years there would be many trios trying to exploit the Cole Trio's demonstrated popularity.

The trio did more radio work—four weeks on Mutual's "Advertisements in Rhythm" and a couple of appearances on Orson Welles's show. They also continued to practice, never allowing their steady work or their success to make them lazy. Besides, they so enjoyed playing together that practicing didn't seem like work. "They take a tune, learn the melody," wrote Barry Ulanov. "Then the three boys sit around and figure out melodic variations, the harmonic complement thereof and Nat writes down the notes. To Oscar, the pianist-leader may say, 'You take this,' to Johnny a similar direction. Then, with voicing established, chorus patterns set, solos assigned, they set to work to make all stick. In half a day, a Cole Trio arrangement or original is established and made permanent in their repertory."

They recorded more of that repertory in 1944, including "The Man I Love," "Body and Soul," "Prelude in C Sharp Minor," "What Is This Thing Called Love?" "After You Get What You Want," "Look What You've Done to Me," "Easy Listenin' Blues," "There I've Said It Again," and more. Capitol also released their first album. By the fall they had enough records in jukeboxes and homes to undertake an ambitious tour. They went with Benny Carter and his orchestra, who were also managed by Carlos Gastel (whose fortunes, needless to say, had risen with the trio's). The guarantee for the trio was $1,750 a week.

The tour opened at the black Howard Theater in Washington, D.C., on September 1. According to Barry Ulanov, who reviewed the first show, there were some kinks yet to be smoothed out—primarily in pacing so as to avoid awkward pauses between numbers. But the music was superb. "Nat Cole and his inspired cohorts, Oscar Moore and Johnny Miller, captivated the audience with the inevitable 'Straighten

Up,' 'Can't See For Lookin',' 'I'm Lost,' 'I Realize Now.' 'All for You,' and a varied choice from the King's rich repertoire. Only thing I missed was a more generous display of the Cole piano, one of the top-ranking jazz keyboard styles."

Cole was indeed doing more singing. Partly it was in response to public demand. Ballads became very popular during the war years—love songs expressed the pain of separation that befell so many families and couples in love. Ballads were the most often played selections on jukeboxes and no doubt helped the growth of that young industry. Ballads were the songs most often requested on radio call-in shows. White singers like Frank Sinatra and Bing Crosby and Perry Como became famous for their renditions of ballads, and eventually even a couple of black singers captured the crossover white audience with their soulful singing. One was Billy Eckstine. The other was Nat King Cole.

In 1944, however, many whites found something improper about a black man singing a love song. This attitude was a vestige of earlier times, when blacks were considered subhuman and thus incapable of human emotions like love. Sissle and Blake as well as Miller and Lyles had been among the first to break the taboo against showing uncomic love between blacks onstage by including a song called "Love Will Find a Way" in *Shuffle Along* in 1920. Noble Sissle later told William Bolcom and Robert Kimball, authors of *Reminiscing with Sissle and Blake,* "On opening night in New York this song had us more worried than anything else in the show. We were afraid that . . . we'd be run out of town. . . . Imagine our amazement when the song was not only beautifully received, but encored." More than twenty years later, most whites had come to a more sympathetic view of blacks as human beings, but that didn't mean they were prepared to let white women listen to black men crooning love songs. For several years Nat Cole's and Billy Eckstine's velvet voices reached primarily black ears.

Cole's voice seemed uniquely suited to ballad singing. Smoky, slightly hoarse, even gravelly, it was not particularly strong. In fact, the story goes that a doctor in the audience once advised him to go home to bed and "take care of that throat." Nat himself said his voice was "nothing to be proud of. It runs maybe two octaves in range. I guess it's the hoarse, breathy noise that some like." More than the voice quality itself was

Cole's style. Billy Eckstine once said that Cole "took a style and made a voice of it." There was a sincerity in Cole's singing that came through; he never just sang a song, he felt it. He was very particular about his songs. They had to express genuine feeling, and he had to be able to sing them as though he meant them. He liked to live with a song for a while before he sang it for an audience or recorded it. Geri Branton remembers, "He used to tell me about the songs he was doing, talk about them as if they were stories. They had to have personal meaning to him." By the time he recorded a song, it had become his own statement. "I consider myself an interpreter of songs rather than a singer," he'd say. The public responded to his sincerity.

"His type of delivery appealed," says Benny Carter. People bought Cole's records because they expressed their own feelings. People flocked to see Cole in person for the same reason. Already he was being called, according to Benny Carter, "a sepia Frank Sinatra—unfortunate term."

Thus, when he and the trio went on tour with Benny Carter and his orchestra, Cole was prepared to give the public what they wanted. Few seemed to regret, as Ulanov did, that he didn't do more piano playing.

The Cole-Carter show was at the Royal Theater, Baltimore, September 8, at the Regal in Chicago September 22, at the Paradise Theater in Detroit September 29, at the Plantation Club in St. Louis for three weeks starting October 6, and then at Cleveland's Palace Theater on November 10. From there they went to New York, where on November 17 they opened at the famed Apollo Theater and, according to one reviewer, "knocked that hypercritical audience for a loop." In fact, they were such a smash that they were held over for another week, a very unusual occurrence at the Apollo. Barry Ulanov reviewed this show as well: "This was the show which broke all records for New York's eminent colored house, and no wonder. For it was everything the combination of King Cole, Benny Carter, Savannah Churchill and Jimmie Rogers had been in Washington in September when the package presentation began its six-month tour of the East, and a whole lot more. The pacing was perfect, this time; there were no stage waits, none of the numbers missed fire. From the opening Carter downbeat to the last scream elicited from the women in the audience by Nat Cole, both style and substance characterized this show." Cole, Carter, and company finished out the year at the Loew's State Theater in Times Square, having captured the hearts of both black uptown and white downtown New Yorkers.

Both Cole as leader of the trio and Oscar Moore as a guitarist were winners of *Metronome*'s 1944 Band Poll that year, the first of many times they were to win such year-end polls. The universal reaction seems to have been that in Cole's case it couldn't have happened to a nicer guy. For Benny Carter, he was not only a partner in a highly successful tour but a friend: "He was very nice, very shy." The people at Capitol Records had reason to be effusive, for Cole had helped to put them on the map; but there is a ring of sincerity in the description of him that appeared in an edition of the company's PR publication *The Capitol*: "Cole is conscientious to the extreme; he practices singing and piano regularly, striving to improve both. He's never late on the job, and his personal habits might well be the model for a troop of Boy Scouts. No one in the music business is better liked.... And if hard work and a surging, inexhaustible desire to please are factors responsible, Nat Cole will retain his title throughout 1945."

The Cole-Carter show continued its successful tour in early 1945, traveling from Flint, Michigan, to Utica and Rochester, New York, to Boston, to Newark, to Hartford, to Philadelphia, back to the Loew's State in New York, then to Detroit. Not only at the Apollo Theater but on several other stages during the tour, they broke all-time attendance records; and more than once the two groups split upward of $4,000 a week. By the time the tour ended and both groups returned to Los Angeles, the King Cole Trio was in the big leagues.

The trio played the Orpheum theater twice in the space of the next few months, the quickest return engagement in the history of the theater. They appeared in United Artists' *Breakfast in Hollywood* and received $13,500 for two days' work. They now commanded $4,000 per week when they appeared at the RKO Palace in Columbus, Ohio, and similar large theaters. J. T. Gipson, who had worked briefly as the group's press agent in 1943, was then theatrical editor of the Ohio State *News,* and he went backstage to interview Cole when the trio played the RKO Palace. "The King didn't give out much information," Gipson later recalled, "only that he was making more money than he'd ever made in his life, and was enjoying the hell out of it."

Maybe Cole had had to give up his dream of leading a band, but the money he was making as leader of a trio softened the blow—a lot. He and Nadine bought a house. He bought a new car and proper performing outfits for his group. For a poor black kid from Chicago's South Side, making money was like having Christmas every day; he spent it as fast as it came in. He didn't worry about getting more; in the mid- to late forties there seemed no end to the new opportunities for the King Cole Trio.

They appeared in a slapstick comedy called *See My Lawyer* for Universal, and Cole received credit as one of the music and lyrics writers for his collaboration with Joe Greene on "Man On the Little White Keys." They recorded twenty-four more sides for Capitol in 1945, among them their second big hit. "The Frim Fram Sauce" was another novelty piece, the novelty sufficient to cause a nationally known food products company to inquire about buying the rights to the title. The company was going to market a new meat sauce with that name and display a picture of the King Cole Trio on the bottle. The deal apparently fell through. The trio appeared in a three-minute "soundie" for USA called *Frim Fram Sauce,* presaging by almost four decades the music video.

"Frim Fram Sauce" was at the top of the charts when the trio recorded "Get Your Kicks on Route 66" on March 16, 1946. This was their next big seller. Most of their recordings sold well, and in 1946 they were hired, along with pianist Eddie Duchin, as a summer replacement for Bing Crosby on the Kraft Music Hall radio show. Especially noteworthy about this weekly, Thursday night show was that the trio not only played and sang but were used in the dialogue skits that followed their instrumental and vocal performances—just like white folks!

The trio made another breakthrough that year, playing a white bastion of hedonism called Las Vegas for the first time. But the management of El Rancho seemed to feel that the King Cole Trio should be content just to perform there and not mind being denied access to the casino. Cole and his musicians completed their engagement, but Cole vowed never again to play Las Vegas under such conditions.

In August of that year Cole made his first recording with strings. "The Christmas Song," written by Mel Tormé and Robert Wells, backed by "In the Cool of the Evening," set a new fashion in standard Christmas tunes, selling so well that other popular singers rushed to record it despite the trend away from multiple recordings of the same song. But it was forever after associated primarily with Cole. He loved the song and always regarded it as one of his favorites. He also liked the string choir background and determined to do more such recordings in the future.

In the fall of 1946 the trio were offered their own national radio show, sponsored by Wildroot Cream Oil. The time slot—5:45 P.M. EDT Saturdays—was practically the graveyard in radio, but the show proved popular enough to remain on the air for sixty-eight weeks.

At year's end, Cole and the trio were winners in the small band category in all the major music polls—*Down Beat, Orchestra World, Band Leaders, Metronome, Billboard.* In the *Esquire* poll, Cole was voted number one for piano and number two for vocals, and Moore was voted number one for guitar. Hollywood's swank Trocadero named a room after them—the King Cole Room. Cole received *Metronome*'s Influence of the Year Award, which was presented him on the Wildroot Cream Oil radio show. According to *Metronome,* "After years of somewhat patronizing tolerance of small combinations, theatre and night club bookers, talent men for record companies, and the public in general, suddenly discovered that three men could make just as appealing music as a big band and that it often pays off to concentrate on quality rather than on quantity." Among the small groups that the trio had influenced were, on the West Coast, the Vivien Garry, Red Callender, and Page Cavanaugh trios, the Lucky Thompson and Eddie Beal quartets; in New York, the Buddy Weed, Herman Chitson, and Dardanelle trios and the Joe Mooney Quartet. Added *Metronome,* "At least one group, the Three Blazers which is led by Oscar Moore's brother Johnny, achieved some popularity with records on which every nuance of Nat's voice and piano were as closely reproduced as possible by Charlie Brown. And considering the sudden outbreak of black-rimmed glasses in the Apple, there are many kids who are trying to look like him as well."

In retrospect, however, the most important event of 1946 for Nat King Cole had nothing to do with music: It was the year he met Maria.

3

Maria

MARIA Hawkins was born in the Roxbury section of Boston in the early 1920s (in 1984 her and Nat's son, Kelly, said she was "about sixty-two"), the second daughter of a mail carrier and his wife. In those days civil service positions were among the highest careers to which blacks who were not preachers, teachers, or doctors could aspire, and the Hawkinses were solidly middle-class. Maria was baptized in the Episcopal Church and was further blessed with the fair skin that went a long way toward ensuring her an easier life than darker-skinned girls, no matter what the circumstances of their birth. When Maria was about two, her mother died giving birth to her third daughter, Carol. For a time, Mingo Hawkins tried raising Charlotte, Maria, and Carol alone; but when Maria was seven or eight he apparently decided that the two older girls needed the guidance of a strong woman. From then on they spent the winter months with their father's sister.

"Mother was raised by Dr. Charlotte Hawkins Brown," says Kelly

Cole. "This woman was only nineteen-years-old when she started the first black prep school. It was 1902—twenty years before women could vote. That's some determination. Mom is very much like her." Dr. Brown, granddaughter of a slave, was a singular woman. She had honorary degrees from Wellesley College and Brown University and was the first black on the national board of the YWCA. The school she founded was Palmer Memorial Institute in Sedalia, North Carolina, and was supported by wealthy white New Englanders, principally the Galen Stones, Charles Elliott, and Alice Freeman Palmer, after whom the school was named. In her biography of her husband, Maria wrote that her aunt, whom the family called Lottie, traveled to Europe long before most other blacks did and that she had written an etiquette book called *The Correct Thing.*

Maria recalls having a pampered childhood in some ways—maids to plait her pigtails, a telephone when most people did not have them, bountiful Christmases, riding in a private Pullman car when she and her sister traveled with their aunt. She remembers, too, that important people visited her aunt—Eleanor Roosevelt, W. E. B. Du Bois, Langston Hughes, Mary McLeod Bethune. But she also remembers that curtseying properly and learning diction and being the niece of a highly respected woman did not shield her entirely from prejudice. When Maria and other students from Palmer Institute went into town to the Carolina Theater they had to sit in the balcony; the downstairs section was reserved for whites. They were unable to go to the country club or to the fine hotels and restaurants in the area; on the rare occasions when they ventured out of their private Pullman car into a train's dining car, waiters pulled a curtain to segregate them from the white diners.

As a youngster, Maria felt stifled in the comparatively rarified atmosphere in which her aunt lived. Her major outlets from the regimentation imposed upon her, especially after her aunt forbade further outings to the segregated Carolina Theater, were listening to the radio and reading movie magazines. By the time she reached adolescence she had two strong ambitions: She wanted to be rich and she wanted to be in show business. Her family had no problem with the first dream, but they frowned upon the second—nice girls did not go into show business. When Maria remained firm in her resolve, her family insisted that she at least complete her education.

On graduation from Palmer Memorial Institute, Maria did attend Boston Clerical College for three years, working nights with Sabby Lewis's orchestra. She then worked in Washington, D.C., at Howard University as secretary to the purchasing agent. But after that she refused to put off the pursuit of her dream any longer. She went to New York. Band leader Benny Carter was one of the first to hire her: "She sang with my orchestra in the early years, at the Savoy Ballroom. She went by the name Marie Winter." (During her singing career, Maria called herself Marie, and people in the music business who remember her then still call her Marie.)

In 1943 Maria married Spurgeon Neal Ellington, a lieutenant in the army air corps who was a member of the legendary black 332d Fighter Group. Henceforth, Maria's stage name was Marie Ellington, which caused a certain amount of confusion when she went to work for Duke Ellington. Every time reporters and critics wrote about her, they felt constrained to mention that she was no relation to the Duke.

By the time she joined Duke Ellington's band, the Duke was a major star and had money enough to hire young women singers essentially as window dressing. Maria joined the band as one of four female singers in 1944. The others were Joya Sherrill, Kay Davis, and Rosita Davis. In his book *Duke Ellington,* published in 1946, Barry Ulanov wrote, "Rosita Davis did not stay with the band very long, and Marie Ellington (no relation of the Duke's) combined Rosita's duties with her own. Though all the duties didn't add up to much, it was enough to show Marie as an able girl who did as much as possible with meager assignments, usually with a pronounced New England accent. Like Kay and Joya, though in a very different way, Marie is unusually attractive. All are fair, Kay with light, Marie and Joya with black hair. Kay's is a kind of baby face, bright and cute; Joya's much like that, though more mischievous-looking; and Marie's is one that shows a sophistication matching her clothing."

While Maria pursued her singing career, her husband was fighting the war. He flew combat missions with his fighter group in Italy and was awarded the Distinguished Flying Cross. In 1945 he finished his tour of duty and returned to the United States and his base at Tuskegee, Alabama. He had just visited Maria in New York when he was killed during a routine training flight in Tuskegee on December 10, 1945.

Maria, now a young widow, continued her singing career, remaining with Duke Ellington another few months. But she was not content with the orchestra, perhaps agreeing with Ulanov that she wasn't getting much chance to develop her talents. She says she began planning to leave Ellington and that when he found out he fired her. In the late spring of 1946, Joe Howard, manager of the Club Zanzibar at Broadway and Forth-ninth Street, hired her as a single, singing two songs per show on the club's bill. She was on the same bill as the Mills Brothers. When the Mills Brothers quit, Maria learned that a group from California, the King Cole Trio, was coming in to replace them. "Who's the King Cole Trio?" Maria wanted to know.

When she found out who they were, she wasn't particularly impressed. But Nat Cole was impressed with her. In her book, Maria says that he saw her first from backstage while she was singing, asked who she was, and commented, "If she looks as good from the front as she does [from] behind . . ." Eddie "Rochester" Anderson formally introduced them, and forever after Nat and Maria referred to him as the instigator of their relationship. Nat apparently didn't need much instigating. He would stand backstage every night and watch her. He began to send champagne to her dressing room. He started driving her home after the last show. Nat Cole, married man, Boy Scout of the music business, was in love.

He and Nadine had been married about nine years by then. She was in her late thirties, he in his late twenties. They had been unable to have children, which Nat keenly regretted, and perhaps that had driven a wedge between them. Another possibility is that, like so many other couples, they were unable to adjust to changing circumstances in their lives: close and mutually supportive when they were poor and Nat was an unknown, they may have found that they had little to share once Nat became successful. All Nadine says is, "He had been on the road. While the cat's away the mice will play." Physically, according to Geri Branton, Maria and Nadine were very much alike, although "Nadine was a little more conventional and not as educated or sophisticated."

Maria's education and sophistication appealed to Cole, as did her beauty. Geri Branton says he told her, "I've never seen a black woman who spoke so well, who dressed so well, who carried herself the way she did." And so he pursued Marie Ellington. At first she rebuffed his advances. She says she did so mainly out of a sense of propriety. But when he offered his ticket to the Joe Louis–Billy Conn fight, all sense of propriety left her. She accepted, and the romance bloomed. He eventually got around to telling her that he was married; she says some girlfriends had told her a few days earlier. That didn't stop him from asking her, on the spur of the moment, to accompany the trio to Indianapolis, nor her from going.

In Indianapolis, Cole sent Maria shopping, for, she says, she had not even brought a toothbrush. She bought several outfits and enjoyed the feeling of being able to buy whatever she fancied.

The trio played for a standing room only audience at the English Theater, and the *Indianapolis Tribune* critic was laudatory, comparing the group to both the Budapest String Quartet and Salvador Dali: "The King Coles take musical phrases as familiar as conversational gadgets like 'Well, whaddya know.' They scramble those phrases like musical quotations, just as Mr. Dali scrambles familiar sights into weird, surrealistic designs. And they do all these things with humorous intent, which is best expressed by Mr. Cole himself, pianist and more than vocalist. Mr. Cole's engaging manner—easy singing and expressive look—in popular songs may obscure his great talent for comedy. I hope and believe he wrote the lines, as the program said he wrote the music, for the ditty that ran:

> Corned beef has its cabbage;
> Mother has Machree.
> Everyone has someone,
> But all I've got is me,"

Even as he sang the ditty, Cole must have been thinking that it no longer applied to him—if indeed he'd ever felt it did. When the group returned from Indianapolis to New York, Cole asked Maria if she would marry him providing he could get a divorce from Nadine. Maria said yes.

Nadine learned of the affair by accident. "I went to New York to say hello and . . . found out about it," she says. "Yes, it was difficult, but I think I took it pretty well." Others did not. Maria's family were horrified. Cole was a married man and a musician besides. Even Maria's older sister, Charlotte, who'd swooned over Cole long before Maria knew who he was, disapproved of the relationship. Maria's Aunt Lottie was adamant that the affair must end. No doubt the family found several other things about Cole objectionable. He was a dark-skinned, Southern-born Baptist with only a high school education—hardly an ideal suitor for Maria. Such considerations may also have given Maria pause. The romantic view is that she loved Nat enough to overlook them. The cynical view is that she knew she could realize a perfectly natural aspiration through him—as Mrs. Nat King Cole, she could be rich.

Whether or not Maria had dollar signs in her eyes, they were present in the eyes of another who objected to Nat's and Maria's marrying. Carlos Gastel reminded Cole that California had community property laws and that if he divorced Nadine he stood to lose sixty thousand dollars. In her book Maria states that a "certain bandleader" in New York was also against the relationship and telephoned Gastel to come to New York to try to talk Nat out of divorcing Nadine; but she does not say who or why.

Oscar Moore and Johnny Miller were also unhappy. Says Geri Branton, "The members of his trio didn't want him to divorce Nadine and marry Maria. They told him she was not for him." The advent of Maria disrupted the close relationship the three men enjoyed. Writing of the times after the shows at the Zanzibar closed, Maria noted, "I don't know whatever happened to poor Oscar and Johnny, but pretty soon it got to be just Nat taking me home." Her attitude toward the two in that statement sounds patronizing, and based on reports of the way she dealt with later members of the trio she may have had that attitude back in 1946. She considered Cole the star and seemed to regard his sidemen as veritable lackeys. They didn't like it or her.

It is possible that Moore and Miller were feeling unhappy around that time for other reasons. More and more, Cole was emerging as the star of the trio because of his vocalizing. His sidemen may have felt, and with good reason, that the group's instrumentals should not be overshadowed. It was their instrumentalizing so perfectly together that had made their musical relationship satisfying for nearly ten years. Moore and Miller were superb musicians and proud of it; they wanted to continue to develop musically. As backup musicians for the voice of Nat King Cole, they felt professionally stalled.

Cole may have shared their feelings. Or he may simply have wished to keep peace in the trio. Whatever the reason, he announced in early 1947 that his first aim had always been not to play music for the most people but to play the best music for those who would listen and accordingly that on their next concert tour the trio would play "more serious music." Reported columnist Joey Sasso in his review of the trio's concert at D'Jais in Secaucus, New Jersey, in late January 1947, "Actually the concert represents to Nat the final casting aside of cheap commercialism. Too long, he feels, has the group hidden its true instrumental talents under a slick polish of novelty songs which are sure to catch the public fancy. From here on in, musicianship will stand on its own merits, and even Capitol Records will see that at least half of all King Cole discs are real jazz."

Mortimer Manville Ruby was hired as road manager for the tour, which took the trio from the Apollo in New York in early February to Hartford, Detroit, Columbus, Cleveland, Cincinnati, Chicago, and back to Detroit. They played across the North and East through the spring, then returned to the West Coast for engagements at the Million Dollar Theater, the Lincoln Theater, the Orpheum, and the Trocadero. Then they went East again. The concert tour did not fulfill Cole's promise to include more serious music. Divided into three parts, each performance featured primarily Cole vocals in the first and last sections with instrumentals in the middle. Reviewing the show at the Chicago Opera House in the early fall of 1947, Don C. Haynes of *Down Beat* complained, "Middle section of the concert was the serious portion, and it pointed up the most debatable thing about the affair. The concert should have been more of a legitimate concert, that is, with more original and serious music than included here. As it was, Nat changed the original program to insert a novelty, 'All I've Got Is Me,' in the place of the more serious 'Chant of the Blues.' Though it brought plenty of laughs, was quite effective, it destroyed the seriousness of this 'concert' part of the evening. Nat explained afterward that the concert tour was thrown at them so fast, and dates arranged so quickly, that he and Oscar and Johnny hadn't had time to prepare half the serious stuff they had wanted to include. . . . But the concert tour has been in preparation, musically at least, for a year."

Nor had the group's recording for Capitol that year been "at least half jazz." The vast majority had been Cole vocals, including a couple of sides with strings and no participation by Moore and Miller. Cole's rendition of Deke Watson's "For Sentimental Reasons" had, along with "The Christmas Song," launched him as a singer into the mainstream of American popular music. Naturally, audiences on the concert tour wanted to hear the ever more famous voice.

By the time the trio played the Opera House in Chicago, Oscar Moore had given his notice. Many people blame Maria for his quitting, and Maria herself claims responsibility. She believed that Cole should go out on his own and if he weren't ready to do that yet, at least he should renegotiate the contracts he held with his sidemen. In her opinion, they were taking far too large a percentage, given that Cole was the real star. "There were weeks," she said in her book, "when Oscar was earning as much as $1,600 to $1,800."

She had considerable influence with Cole. Not only was she beautiful and classy in his eyes, she was also smart in areas where he felt lacking. He was keenly aware of his lack of education and, legend has it, of his transplanted Southern dialect. Although Nadine Coles says he had no problem with diction when he was married to her, there is evidence that his enunciation did need improvement. Arnold Shaw reported that Cole actually went to a speech therapist, but by most accounts his only speech therapist was Maria. Whoever is responsible for his careful diction, legions of record listeners would be grateful. "He had perfect pronunciation," says Benny Carter. "You never had to turn around and ask, 'What did he say? What did he say?'"

Maria says she helped him to dress more conservatively and thus more acceptably as well.

Cole also did not consider himself a businessman. He never budgeted money and didn't think much about it, as long as it kept coming in. Maria says he was a soft touch and forever lending to friends money that would never be repaid. She also felt that he was too trusting. She was willing to take charge of his affairs, and Cole was willing to let her. Kelly Cole believes that these qualities in Maria also attracted Cole. "In the research I've done, I've found out something about Dad that I never knew before," says Kelly. "The legend is that he was a simple, happy-go-lucky type. But he had a shrewdness that never manifested itself in an ugly or manipulative manner but in matters of choice. One can see that especially in his choice of wives. He was very much in love with the women he married, but they were also women who could help him—at *that* time. Both were connected with music, both understood his talent. Mom is very practical, very grounded in reality." When Cole met Maria, he was beginning to make big money, acquiring a coterie of hangers-on, poised on the brink of all the pitfalls that present themselves to unwary new stars. He believed he needed someone like Maria to keep his feet on the ground, to protect him from being used.

Irving Ashby, who replaced Oscar Moore, doesn't believe that Maria was the major reason for Moore's quitting. He points out that Moore's brother, Johnny, had formed a trio—Johnny Moore and His Three Blazers—and that from then on Oscar had been looking for a way to join his brother. "He was looking for an alibi, a reason to leave Nat and go with his brother," says Ashby. "Every time he started to quit, Nat would raise his pay or give him a bonus. So then Marie comes in, and she provided the alibi. So she was indirectly responsible for Oscar's quitting, but in another way she wasn't. He just used that as an excuse to do what he'd been wanting to do—play with his older brother."

Moore still had enough loyalty to Cole not to leave him in the lurch. He stayed with the trio until Cole found a suitable replacement. In fact, he was with the trio when they celebrated their tenth anniversary with a concert at Carnegie Hall in October. But when he was satisfied that Cole would be ably served by Irving Ashby he departed without regret.

Ashby had grown up in the same Boston neighborhood as Maria and had known her from the time she was about fourteen. He had taught himself to play the guitar. "My family was loaded with musicians and people in show business," he says. "Fats Waller used to come by the house all the time." Ashby's father was superintendent of the apartment building where they lived, and when he was old enough, young Ashby began to tend the furnaces at night. While attending Roxbury Memorial High School, he also played guitar at a nightclub at Revere Beach. "There was no time for homework," he says. He later played with the Sheloh Khall Electric Choir, the Eddie Watson Trio, Lionel Hampton, and Phil Moore. Married to a schoolteacher and himself an army veteran, Ashby was a mature performer who took seriously his new job with the King Cole Trio:

"Naturally I couldn't just come in and take over, so I had to travel with them for a while and stand in the wings and watch Oscar play and listen to him play and try to get an idea of his style, so when he did leave I could come in and have an idea of what was expected of me. In those days we rode on trains—there was very little flying. Everyone had their drawing room. Oscar and I had a drawing room. I had a clipboard—I was almost like a reporter, asking him questions—'What do you do on this song?' etc. I didn't want to sound exactly like him, but I wanted to be as close to his style as possible so that Nat's image wouldn't be hurt. The whole thing kind of amused Oscar."

Ashby entered Cole's employ as of September 27, 1947. Here is the letter of agreement he signed:

September 23, 1947

Mr. Irving Ashby
1041 West 36th Place
Los Angeles 7, California

Dear Mr. Ashby:

Inasmuch as I am desirous of obtaining your services to perform as guitarist for the King Cole Trio, the following is to serve as an agreement between us.

It is understood that you are to commence your employment on September 27, 1947. You are to receive a compensation of $150.00 weekly from this date on in preparation of your active participation as a musician with the King Cole Trio.

It is further understood that commencing with the day that you shall be a playing and active member of the King Cole Trio your salary is to be $350.00 per week. The above stipulated sum is to be paid to you weekly for forty eight (48) weeks of the year.

In the event I should be desirous of discharging you and wish to terminate this agreement, I shall compensate you with four (4) weeks salary at the rate of $150.00 weekly.

You hereby agree that you will not render your services to anyone else and shall be under my exclusive employ for a period of one (1) year, and that you shall perform for me on radio, motion pictures, personal appearances and all other fields of the entertainment business for the above mentioned price unless American Fedaration (sic) of Musicians scale exceeds that price.

If the above meets with your approval, kindly sign the space for acceptance provided below.

Sincerely,

_____

Nat "King" Cole

By (Carlos Gastel)
Attorney in Fact

ACCEPTED AND AGREED TO:

_____

Irving Ashby

The terms of the letter were far less lucrative than those under which Oscar Moore had worked, but then Ashby still had to prove himself with the group.

Ashby made his U.S. debut with the trio in late October in his hometown, Boston. According to the *Baltimore Afro-American,* "Boston's talented Irving Ashby, replacing Oscar Moore on the electric guitar, acquitted himself brilliantly in his debut with the Cole outfit after only two previous performances with Cole and Miller in Toronto. Executing in an unusually fast and clean cut style, Ashby proved himself a superb musician with all the refinement and sensitive tonal quality of the finished artist. . . . he plays in a highly relaxed and sure manner, delivering his solos with the clarity and colorful variation of a master."

With or without Oscar Moore, the King Cole Trio maintained its popularity. It carried off top honors in the small band category in all the major music polls for 1947 and continued to embody the standard by which all similar groups were judged. Cole faced 1948 confident that his group's sound was intact. He was confident, too, that his personal life would bring him a happiness that he had not known in years. He now had success and money and would soon have a classy wife to match.

His interlocutory divorce from Nadine, obtained in 1947, became final in the spring of 1948. "One of the clauses in the settlement was that if she remarried, she wouldn't get anything," says Geri Branton. "She got a house . . . and about one hundred and fifty a week. If she'd had a black lawyer, she would have cleaned up." Nadine remained in Los Angeles until the early 1960s, when she moved to St. Louis. Immediately after the divorce, she cut all ties to the people she'd known when she was married to Nat. "After he married Maria, Nadine just dropped all her friends," says Geri Branton.

Nat and Maria were married on Easter Sunday, March 28, 1948, in a Baptist ceremony. Maria, whom Nat called Skeez, would have preferred an Episcopal church wedding, but since Nat was divorced they would have had to get special permission from the bishop, and that would have taken more time than they cared to wait. So they were married at Abyssinian Baptist Church in Harlem by the Reverend Adam Clayton Powell, Jr., who was also a Democratic congressman from New York (and whose father, the Reverend Adam Clayton Powell, Sr., was a friend of her family's, according to Maria).

Harlem historians averred that the $17,500 wedding and reception were the most elaborate since 1923, when May Robinson, granddaughter of hair straightener millionairess Madame C. J. Walker, had a wedding that cost $45,000. *Life* carried a full spread on the event. Guests included actor Canada Lee, actor and dancer Bill "Bojangles" Robinson, pianist Hazel Scott (then Mrs. Adam Clayton Powell, Jr.), bandleader Andy Kirk, and singers Nellie Lutcher and Sarah Vaughan. Bridesmaids included Mrs. Mercer Ellington, wife of the Duke's son, who had earlier given a shower for Maria, and Mrs. Bill Robinson. Maria's father gave her away; her older sister, Charlotte Charity, was matron of honor; her younger sister, Carol Lane, was a bridesmaid; and Carol's small daughter, Carol (called Cookie), was the flower girl. Maria's Aunt Lottie, Dr. Charlotte Hawkins Brown, still did not approve of the marriage, but she was in attendance and had given Maria her gown—an off-shoulder brocaded satin with long sleeves and a white shawl collar. Eddie Coles was Nat's best man, and the rest of his family were there as well, though somewhat overshadowed by the luminaries.

The evening before, the bride- and groom-to-be had been barely speaking, Maria wrote in her book. Nat had been out all night the previous night at a stag party at Al and Dick's on West Fifty-fourth Street. When she learned what took place at stag parties, Maria refused to participate in the wedding rehearsal. At the wedding reception held at the Moderne Room of the Belmont Plaza Hotel at Forty-ninth Street and Lexington Avenue, Nat got "a wee bit smashed," she says, and didn't remember a thing about their wedding night.

Since Nat was not a heavy drinker as a rule, one wonders why he got drunk twice in so short a space of time. Getting drunk at one's own stag party is understandable; getting drunk at your own wedding reception is another matter. He may have been reacting to the sheer lavishness of the wedding, a display that was just too much for him. He may also have been reacting to the apparent disapproval of him on the part of Maria's family and to Maria's seeming cold-shouldering of his own family. Many believe that she looked down on the Coles of Chicago and made little effort to hide her apparent disdain for their dark skins, their ungrammatical speech, and their lack of sophistication. It must have been painful for Nat to feel ashamed of his family and ashamed of himself for feeling that way.

Nat managed to stay sober during the second reception. This one was staged by Aunt Lottie at her home in Sedalia, North Carolina, where Maria and Nat visited on their way to their Mexican honeymoon. Aunt Lottie planned the reception, invited all the notables in the area, oversaw the final arrangements, then left town. She herself did not attend the reception.

Nat and Maria spent their honeymoon in Mexico City and Acapulco. They were accompanied by *Ebony* photographer Griffith Davis, and the magazine ran a feature on the honeymoon in its August 1948 issue. While in Mexico, Nat received a wire from Hollywood: his recording of "Nature Boy" was the number one hit in the United States.

Nature
Boy

LIKE any other successful singer, then as now, Cole was besieged by would-be songwriters who assured him or, if they could not get to him personally, those around him that their song could be a hit if only he would record it. According to Maria in 1954, "I don't know how they find out, but before he's in town for a few minutes they know his hotel room number. When we are not plagued with visits we are plagued with phone calls. I am not complaining, mind you. I know that's his life and in his position it is something to be expected. But it does wear you thin. It's so difficult to convince these song sellers that any singer's major source of material is through the song publisher's office."

Cole had learned to avoid them as much as possible, but on occasion an amateur songwriter did get through to him. In one case the songwriter was also a reporter who began his interview by presenting Cole with a song he'd written. But the most celebrated case in Cole's career—and among the most heralded in the history of American popular music—was that of the barefoot yogi from Brooklyn and his Asiatic tone poem.

In June 1947 the King Cole Trio was doing a stint at a theater in Los Angeles (sources differ as to whether it was the Orpheum, the Million Dollar, or the Lincoln) when one evening a bearded long-haired man wearing an old drab gray smock appeared at the backstage door and asked to see Nat King Cole's manager. The doorman dutifully located Mort Ruby, but Ruby, who was accustomed to fending off amateur songwriters, said that he was busy. The man would not be put off. He had taken his song to Johnny Mercer, at Capitol Records, and Mercer had suggested that he show it to Cole. He hung around the stage door until Ruby walked by and pressed a soiled sheet of music into his hand, saying it was a song he had written for Cole. To get rid of the man, Ruby said he would see what he could do and asked the man his name. "Eden Ahbez" was the reply. The song he was peddling was called "Nature Boy Suite." (One version of the legend holds that Ahbez submitted two songs, the other being "I'm a Real Gone Yogi," and that Cole had immediately rejected the first.)

According to Maria Cole, Ruby gave the music to Nat and thought little more about the matter until several days later when Cole, having looked over the song, suggested to his manager that it might be the kind of "Jewish song" Ruby had been urging him to record. As a result of the Nazi atrocities against the Jews during the war, there was considerable pro-Jewish sentiment in the United States, and Ruby felt that Cole should record a song that somehow expressed that sentiment. Ruby looked over the song and agreed that it was Jewish sounding. However, in his opinion the lyric was a little far out. And that title! The two went on to discuss other things.

A few days later, Ahbez returned to the theater to inquire about the status of his song. This time he managed to collar Cole's valet, to whom, according to Maria Cole, he promised 50 percent of the sale price if the man would use his influence to get Cole to record it. Maria says that Ahbez was in the habit of using this tactic to get his song considered and in the course of trying to sell it promised several hundred percent of it to various people. Cole's valet said he would see what he could do.

The King Cole Trio finished their engagement at the theater and moved on to the Beaucage, a small club on the Sunset Strip one flight up from a restaurant. Carlos Gastel had just taken over its management. Gastel's fortunes had risen with the trio's. He now had a busy artists management firm, General Artists Corporation, and a number of successful acts. Nellie Lutcher was playing at the club when Gastel took over. In her book, Maria Cole says that Gastel put his hands over his ears "to shut out the sound of a woman furiously playing the piano and singing rather loudly." Gastel, according to Maria, found out how much Lutcher was making and instructed Mort Ruby to pay her off and tell her to go home. Then, the King Cole Trio moved in.

Nellie Lutcher disputes Maria's account. In fact, after Maria's biography of Nat came out, she considered taking some action over the allegation. She insists that she was not fired, that in fact Gastel was then her manager also. "The man Gastel was responsible for my working at the Beaucage. That he had someone pay me and tell me to go home . . . it just did not happen." Lutcher knew Nat from his early days in Los Angeles; in 1948, a year after the incident at the Beaucage is supposed to have occurred, Lutcher was a guest at Nat and Maria's wedding, and in 1950 Carlos Gastel would bring her and Nat together to record two sides for Capitol. It is therefore unlikely that she would have been treated the way Maria said she had. Lutcher feels that Maria Cole did not like her because she had known Cole when he was married to Nadine. "I heard from various friends that anyone who was in the picture before she came along got the same kind of treatment." Obviously, that's a subjective observation.

During the Cole Trio's second show on opening night at the Beaucage, Cole learned that Irving Berlin was in the house. He suggested to Gastel that it would be a good time to "break in that piece of Jewish material." According to legend, the trio finished the set and before Cole could reach his dressing room Berlin had offered to buy the song. Cole explained that he didn't know anything about it, not even where Eden Ahbez was.

Berlin's interest further piqued Cole's, and Cole directed his people to find Ahbez. They searched without success. Cole continued to include the song in performances and was pleased with the response the song elicited. In August the trio had a recording session scheduled for Capitol, and he casually included a rendition of the song during the session. (Recording sessions were more informal in those days, involving far less preparation, and the King Cole Trio's recording sessions were particularly casual—they did not rehearse at all, and there was seldom more than one "take" on a tune). The producer of the session was immediately moved by the song and declared it great in its subtlety. He, too, urged that the author be found. Mort Ruby now began to search seriously.

At last Cole's people located Eden Ahbez. Legend has it that he was found under the first *L* in the big HOLLYWOOD sign in the Hollywood Hills that greets the approaching visitor. If he was not actually there, he was in a similar location. According to some sources, he was not living under the *L* but under a peach tree at a house on Avenel Street, in the garden of a woman who charged him $3.75 a week for its use. With his wife, who was expecting their first child, he slept in a double sleeping bag, ate fruit and nuts, and communed with the universe.

Brooklyn-born, Ahbez was the son of a Scottish father and an American mother. He spent most of his early years in an orphanage. An "inner urge" stimulated him to seek after a higher truth, and he crossed the country on foot not once but eight times by his thirty-fifth year. Finding his higher truth in Tujunga Canyon in California, he settled on the West Coast. There he took the name eden ahbez, disdaining capital letters for words other than Life, Happiness, Love, and Nature.

Roaming around the streets of Hollywood spouting Oriental philosophy, he had become known in the area as the Yogi and the Hermit. While some people avoided him, others were charmed by him, among them his wife, the former Anna Jacobson. The first time he saw her in a restaurant in downtown L.A., he knew she was destined to be his wife. He followed her to a bus stop and handed her a note with his name and address. Anna, who was "unhappy in her job," responded to the overture of the barefoot man, whose getup rather appealed to her. They were married in a fruit orchard by a black minister, and apparently Anna took happily to her new husband's life-style, which would not be widely practiced until the 1960s, some fifteen years later.

Ahbez had long been a writer of poems, and he had written the words to the song he eventually presented to Cole back in 1944. According to some sources, the song was actually part of a suite in which six popular and classical form tunes are linked. Ahbez studied piano for a year in order to put the material to music. When Mort Ruby found him, Ahbez believed he would actually hear his song on record and sung by Nat King Cole, but it was not to happen quite yet. After going to considerable trouble to find the yogi, Ruby learned that Capitol executives had decided that the lyric was too subtle to be commercial and had shelved the song.

Cole continued to believe in the song and to include it at an occasional concert or club date. After it had sold more than a million copies, in August 1948 a writer for the *Portland* (Oregon) *Journal* recalled, "Nat offered the song about the nuts and berry boy when he was here more than a year ago but then it was an unknown and the applause was restrained. Proves what build-up can do."

Four months and ten recording sessions later, in December, Cole went to a recording studio in New York to do some songs that had been arranged by Peter Rugolo and that called for lusher instrumentals than had backed him up in earlier recordings—strings and a full orchestral treatment by the Frank De Vol orchestra. Among the songs he recorded that day, December 20, were "Lost April," "Lillette," "Monday Again," "Lulu Belle," and "It's So Hard to Laugh (It's So Easy to Cry)." Nat particularly liked "Lost April" from the movie *The Bishop's Wife* starring Cary Grant, Loretta Young, and David Niven. He also still liked the Jewish song that he'd recorded back in August but which had not been released. He showed it to Rugolo, who liked it, too, and who decided to try it with full orchestra. The song, according to legend, was a last-minute addition to the recording session, the musicians playing after a few instructions from Rugolo as to what introduction and effects he wanted. On hearing it, the Capitol executives who'd earlier thought the song's lyrics too subtle liked the new arrangement of "Nature Boy" enough to put it on the flip side of "Lost April" and to schedule it for release on March 29, 1948. Although Ahbez didn't want his name on the label to be in capital letters, explaining that no human being rated capitals, the record company printed his name in capital letters. According to newspaper reports, Capitol did, however, pay him the rather odd sum he had requested as an advance, based on his belief in numerology. The actual sum was not reported.

Hearing "Nature Boy" with strings, Cole grew excited about the song and its possibilities as a hit. In association with Gastel, he set up a publishing firm, Crestview Music, and arranged with another music publisher, Burke & Van Heusen, an affiliate of Edwin H. Morris, to distribute the song. All agreed that it would be a hit, and plans were made to launch it first in New York and to sit on it until the Cole record was released. Ordinarily a new song was published and essentially put up for grabs to anyone who wanted to record it. But Cole and Gastel were so sure this song was perfect for Cole that they defied convention. They insisted that Capitol agree to keep the song under wraps until after the first of the year when the Petrillo ban on all recordings went into effect.

Less than six years after the ban he had imposed in 1942 to 1943, James C. Petrillo and his union, the American Federation of Musicians, were involved in another bitter contract dispute with the record companies. Petrillo had called a strike for January 1, 1948, and the record companies, facing an indeterminate period when they would be unable to produce new recordings, had rushed to get as much material recorded as possible before the strike. That's one reason why Cole and the trio had recorded more than ten times between August and December 1947.

Other recording companies and artists had similarly frantic schedules that fall, and in the rush to get as much music recorded as possible there was a great need for new material. That Cole and Gastel and Capitol succeeded in keeping "Nature Boy" a secret is remarkable, for leaks in the recording business were always numerous and never more so than just before the 1948 Petrillo ban. Peggy Lee wrote "Mañana" and, according to columnist Jack O'Brian, thought she had the only orchestra-accompanied recording as of the Petrillo ban, only to find that another instrumental recording of the song had been made before January 1. The other recording ate only a little into the sales of Lee's own version, however.

The "Nature Boy"/"Lost April" record was delivered to WNEW Radio in New York on March 22, 1948. Music librarian Al Trilling, logging it in, became so excited when he listened to it that he rushed it to disc jockey Jerry Marshall, who was broadcasting his daily Music Hall program at the time. Marshall respected Trilling's opinions, and without hearing it beforehand, put the record on the turntable, announcing to his listeners, "Here's a winner—a song everybody is going to love." It was 2:16 P.M. By the time the four-minute record was over, calls from enthusiastic listeners lit up the station's switchboard. For the next several weeks the song aired at least ten times a day on WNEW, and listeners wanted more. After each playing twenty-five to thirty people called to exclaim over it.

By the time of its formal release on March 29, 1948, the eight lines of lyrics and sixteen bars of music, with vocals by Nat King Cole and piano by *Buddy* Cole, was the biggest song in the country. By the end of May it was the most often played record on jukeboxes from coast to coast. The trade publication *The Cash Box,* in its Automatic Music section, listed the ten top records city by city, and in every city polled, "Nature Boy" was number one—not just in New York, Chicago, and Los Angeles but in Stamford, Connecticut, Dodge City, Kansas, Helena, Montana, Jackson, Mississippi, and Concord, New Hampshire. And not only was "Nature Boy" the top song, but Nat King Cole's rendition of it was the favorite.

A variety of other popular singers had rushed to record their own versions, most without instrumental accompaniment because of the Petrillo ban. Frank Sinatra recorded it a cappella for Columbia with a vocal choir background, Sarah Vaughan sang it a cappella for Musicraft, and Dick Haymes did the same for Decca. Rainbow Records thought to outwit the ban by having Archdale J. Jones sing the song accompanied by Eddy Manson on mouth organ, an instrument that Petrillo did not consider an instrument and that was not covered by the ban. The Harmonicats, who'd had a hit with "Peg o' My Heart," recorded the song for Universal Records. Perry Como's record company, RCA Victor, had wanted him to record the song, but he had refused, saying that Cole's market lead on the tune was too great to overcome.

Como's feeling was becoming more common in the recording industry, where a trend toward fewer recordings was starting. Nat Cole's market lead on "Nature Boy" further stimulated the trend. Although many other singers had recorded the song, his rendition was clearly the best mating of tune and artist, just as Peggy Lee's version of "Mañana" and Vaughn Monroe's of "Ballerina" had been. While other versions of a hit record were inevitable, the tendency after the Petrillo ban was lifted was not to spread new songs among the greatest number of artists and record companies as had been done before.

Cole's version of "Nature Boy" continued to sell at an astounding rate.

Such huge popularity had greeted other records in the past. Most of them had been novelty tunes—"Mañana" (around the same period), "Four Leaf Clover," "Open the Door, Richard" and in the late 1930s, "The Music Goes Round and Round." Public reaction to them had followed the same general trend—initial amusement, obsession, and then complete irritation. The songs enjoyed a meteoric rise and then, suddenly, were falling stars. But "Nature Boy" was different. As "A Reader" wrote to a local black weekly in Los Angeles, "People like the song 'Nature Boy' because it expresses a universal truth. The greatest thing one can learn is to love and be loved. Pure, unselfish love brings more happiness into the world than anything else. This was the weight of the Master's message. All our hearts recognize this fact so we like to hear it expressed even in a simple story."

For Cole, although "Nature Boy" was hardly the first of his records to appeal to the crossover white audience, it was nevertheless gratifying that so many whites were buying a message of universal love sung by a Negro. He was not alone in feeling that way. *The New York Age,* a black newspaper, had reported in late April, "On 42nd Street, between Seventh and Eighth avenues, for instance, the record shops play this number constantly, over and over again. Great crowds gather, some hearing it for the umpteenth time, others just getting to know about it. Many of them head straight inside to buy it. We think that it is an important artistic success and we couldn't help beaming with pride—inside—to hear some of the comments: 'That feller, King Cole, he's colored, isn't he?'"

With "Nature Boy," Cole finally managed a nearly complete crossover to the white market. Except for Billy Eckstine, he would remain unique in this achievement until about 1954, when the advent of rock 'n' roll, so undeniably black-influenced, really began to make the music world more fluid between black and white.

It should be noted that "Nature Boy" did not threaten the traditional white notion of what was proper for blacks to sing. The song was universal in its appeal and did not, directly, present the image of a black crooner being swooned over by a white female listener. In that, the song was a great bridge to the white market for Cole. Having become used to his voice on that song, many white record buyers had no compunction about purchasing the more traditionally romantic ballads that came later.

Eden Ahbez remained "in town" during contract and motion picture negotiations (RKO purchased screen rights to the song, intending to feature it in *The Boy with Green Hair* and to have Cole sing it in the film). But he professed to despise the wealth he would earn from his song—an estimated thirty thousand dollars for 1948 alone—although it is reported that he did buy a car with his first fifteen-hundred-dollar royalty check, which he received in April. Asked what he would do with all his money, he responded, "I will put the money away somewhere where I cannot touch it—maybe some day I will have some use for it. You see, I don't need money at all. I live on three dollars a week. That's what it costs me for my vegetables, fruits, and nuts."

Within a few days of making that statement, Ahbez learned that he might not have any money at all to put away and probably would have to come up with far more than three dollars a week to pay his legal expenses in the plagiarism suit that was brought against him by Herman Yablakoff, whose 1935 Yiddish hit "Schweig Mein Hertz" (Be Calm, My Heart) "Nature Boy" very closely resembled.

Yablakoff was a producer-singer-comedian also known as The Payatz (clown). "Schweig Mein Hertz" was one of the songs in a musical called *Pappirosen* that had played the Second Avenue Theater in New York in 1935. J & J Kammen Music Company, publishers of Jewish songs, had issued the song and was bringing suit on behalf of Yablakoff. Twice before the firm had successfully brought plagiarism suits through their attorney, A. Edward Masters, concerning hits of earlier years: "Isle of Capri" and "Bei Mir Bist Du Schoen" (recorded in 1938 by the Andrews Sisters and the song that "made" the group). The "Nature Boy" suit, brought against Edwin H. Morris & Company as selling agent, asked for no less than one hundred percent of the profits.

After months of litigation, Masters was able to prove that Ahbez could have seen a copy of the song in a Brooklyn music shop. The final settlement gave Kammen and Yablakoff a large share in the royalties.

Ahbez's brush with capitalism did not alter his lifestyle to any appreciable degree. Carol Cole, who was four when her mother died and Nat and Maria adopted her in 1948, recalls, "I have a very clear memory of standing with my father, holding his hand. We were on the corner of Sunset and Vine, right in front of Wallich's Music City, and we were talking to this man who I really thought was Jesus Christ. That man, of course, was Eden Ahbez—forties or fifties in age, long hair and in robes. He really did live under the first *L* in the Hollywood sign. He couldn't have been more perfect for the media. I saw a piece about him in the *Los Angeles Times* around 1977—by his sister-in-law, beautifully written. He continues to live that life. He has not altered from that place." Perhaps the lawsuit against him back in 1948 reinforced his belief that his alternate life-style was preferable to the world of Hollywood hype.

A suit in which Cole was the plaintiff was settled in the same week as J & J Kammen Company brought its suit. Oscar Moore sued Cole for 27½ percent, or $8,250, of the $30,000 in record royalties Cole had collected from Capitol Records since Moore had quit the trio in late October 1947. Cole and Carlos Gastel pointed out that Cole's contract with Capitol gave him personally a cut on sales but not his sidemen. However, Cole had been in the habit of paying bonuses to his musicians, bonuses that had increased Moore's $25,000 salary for 1947 to $57,000. Thus, while there was no contractual bonus agreement, Cole had, in effect, given his musicians a cut, and he and Gastel realized that a court might rule against him in the Moore case. Also, Moore's suit asked for a percentage of all future royalties earned from records made while he was with the trio, and neither Cole nor Gastel looked forward to that kind of complicated bookkeeping. Eventually they settled out of court, and Moore received an undisclosed sum.

Johnny Miller quit the trio that spring. It is not clear exactly why, but perhaps he simply felt the time had come. The trio was not the same anymore. It is also possible that Maria is right to take responsibility for his quitting. No doubt it rankled with her that he was working under the old agreement and making so much more than Ashby. Miller later sued Cole for two weeks' back salary and record royalties. Cole replaced Miller with Joe Comfort, who Cole said was "the peer of any bass player he had ever heard."

While the bassist had never been as crucial to the King Cole Trio sound as the guitarist, the absence of a talented bassist would have been conspicuous. There was a subtlety about the blend of instruments that only the highly trained ear could understand; and yet even an untrained ear would have known something was wrong if Miller had been replaced by a hack. Cole chose a man whose work he knew, who had been an admirer of his for years, and who would have joined the trio in 1942 if he had not been drafted. When he signed with Cole, Comfort was playing with Lionel Hampton, but he couldn't turn down the opportunity to work with a man who was "one of my favorite pianists, along with Art Tatum, Teddy Wilson. He could flip down anybody's piano and get his sound out of it. Just an old, raggedy upright—he could play just two or three bars and I could tell it was him. He had a touch that was unique. The only guy I know who can halfway sound like him is Oscar Peterson—he can kind of get that touch."

Comfort continues, "I used to play at Earl Carrol's up there on Sunset. Nat was playing around the corner on Vine Street at the Radio Room, which was a bowling alley. I'd get off at twelve o'clock, and I used to go in there and sit in with Nat. He told me, 'If I ever need a bass . . .' At that time Wesley Prince was playing bass. When he got drafted, I was supposed to take his place. But then *I* got drafted. That was 1942. That's when he got Johnny Miller. When I joined the trio it was 1948 and they were at the Million Dollar Theater. It was in downtown L.A., and L.A. was jumping then; a big theater where all the bands used to play; I'd played there with Lionel Hampton's band. Johnny Miller didn't give me any advice. I just went in there and started playing. But I'd known Nat for about ten years—not real close but so as we could talk—so I didn't feel strange."

Comfort knew he wouldn't be earning as much as Miller had, but that didn't bother him especially. He understood that things were different now, that the trio was not the same kind of unit as it once had been. Nat was the star. Comfort felt fortunate to be able to play with him.

With his new unit, Cole seemed to do more charity work, a change that was probably less related to his personnel than it was to Maria's influence, charity work being high on the activity list of the black bourgeoisie. On June 12, 1948, the trio was in New York City putting on a show with Thelma Carpenter and other black stars at Abyssinian Baptist Church to raise money for the annual visit by Harlem youngsters to Vermont. They also played a number of benefits in the L.A. area around that time. All the charities and causes for which they performed were "mainstream." Unlike Lena Horne, Paul Robeson (who was his friend), and others, Cole didn't get involved in leftist causes, nor controversial ones. In the forties, the Council on African Affairs, of which Robeson was chairman, co-sponsored with the newspaper *Peoples Daily World,* an appeal for funds to aid black South African drought victims. Cole did not take part in that appeal; nor did he take part in anti-Ku Klux Klan rallies in the forties. He was basically apolitical, for one thing; and for another, he did not want to be associated with controversial causes because they might hamper his career. Such associations might, for example, prevent him from getting bookings at the high-class Ciro's.

The trio was originally booked into the Million Dollar Theater beginning July 6, 1948, and scheduled to go on to Ciro's on the Sunset Strip starting July 16. But Herman D. Hover, Ciro's manager, insisted on no booking at all unless he got the trio first. The Million Dollar Theater management agreed and accepted the combo for the week of August 10. The rearrangement proved to benefit everyone involved. In PR parlance, the trio "brought out the carriage trade at Ciro's," including Prince Mohammed Ali and Princess Hanrede of Egypt, the Louis Jourdans, and Ronald Reagan and Betty Blyth. Although Eden Ahbez failed to show up for opening night as scheduled, telephoning at the last minute to plead a "previous commitment," no one missed him. The packed house was hushed during the two half-hour sessions. Cole favored his audience with a new song, "Portrait of Jennie," by J. Russel Robinson, which brought down the house.

H. D. Hover was planning a film about his club, titled *Ciro's of Hollywood,* and immediately entered into negotiations with Carlos Gastel to feature Cole in it. By the time they completed arrangements, a special part was being written into the script so that Cole would work throughout the picture. Cole's film horizons were expanding rapidly at this time, for simultaneously Gastel was negotiating with a new video film company formed by Harry Grey and Bill Richards to produce a video of the King Cole Trio and Nellie Lutcher.

But for all their popularity the King Cole Trio were still blacks traveling in a predominantly white world, and little time passed between the frequent reminders of their odd and uncomfortable place. During their engagement at Ciro's, Rosetta Tharpe and Artie Graves were denied admittance to the club.

J. T. Gipson, who ran the story in the *California Eagle,* described Graves as a "popular young sportsman," so he was probably not known outside L.A.'s black "sporting" community. But Rosetta Tharpe was. A guitar-playing gospel singer, she had achieved national fame at the celebrated Cotton Club in its downtown Manhattan location a decade or so before. To the headwaiter at Ciro's, however, she was just another Negress. The headwaiter blocked the entrance to the club and informed the couple that Ciro's was "filled up." When Graves protested that they had reservations, the man said there must be some mistake. He became angry and abusive. Graves got an attorney.

When Cole heard about the incident, he told Graves, "This job doesn't mean so much to me that my people have to be insulted when they come to hear us play. I'll be your witness. . . . It doesn't matter how much money you get in suing the place, but this kind of stuff must be broken down!"

This could not have been the first such incident in Cole's experience. Even if it had not happened to him, he knew of similar incidents that had occurred when other black performers were engaged at posh white clubs. Bill Bojangles Robinson had been refused admittance to New York City's Copacabana to see Lena Horne that same year (1948). Lena had issued a statement vowing not to play the Copacabana again while members of her own race were denied the opportunity to see her, although there was nothing she could do to break her contract with the Copa for that particular engagement. Such experiences did not wear well with successful black performers, and perhaps the reactions of Cole and Horne were indicative of an incipient rebellion against such actions on the part of white clubs whose managements believed they were doing black performers a favor by letting them appear. But Cole was a quiet man who preferred to avoid controversy and who was very realistic in his assessment of the boundaries beyond which he, as a black, could not go, no matter how many of his recordings reached number one on the popular charts. One wonders if he would not have kept his feelings about the incident at Ciro's to himself if he had not at the same time been embroiled in another, much larger racial controversy, one that put not only his own dignity but his stature in the eyes of his new bride on the line.

5

"I Am an American Citizen"

BEFORE his marriage to Maria, Cole hadn't been particularly concerned with where he lived. He wanted a comfortable home, a nice home, but he never considered his home a statement of his position. It was Maria who persuaded him that it was not only proper for him to have a home befitting his stardom but also a smart way to invest some of his steadily rising income. So, while they lived in the Watkins Hotel for the first six months of their marriage, they began to look for a house. They looked at more than a dozen houses in Beverly Hills and were received graciously everywhere they went; Nat was asked to sign autographs in several neighborhoods. It's unlikely, however, that most of the residents of these neighborhoods realized that the black couple were seriously househunting.

According to Maria, it was Nat who chose the house they decided to buy. The ivy-covered English Tudor-style red brick home at 401 South Muirfield Road in the Hancock Park section had been built by the late

William Lacey, former president of the Los Angeles Chamber of Commerce; its present owner was one Colonel Henry Ganz. Maria recalls that the moment Nat walked into the front hallway, he declared, "This is it"; and even though she protested that she had not yet seen the kitchen, his mind was made up.

Once they had decided to buy the house, Nat and Maria felt they had to engage in subterfuge, for the Hancock Park area was exclusively white. The real estate agent, Joe Bradfield of Smith and Canaday Real Estate, a black firm, found a "white" purchaser (an extremely light-complexioned black woman) who put a six thousand dollar binder on the eighty-five thousand dollar house. She then transferred her interest to the Coles. When many of the Coles' intended neighbors learned of the transfer, they joined ranks to try to prevent the sale of the house. The hastily formed Hancock Park Property Owners Association elected an attorney who lived in the area as its president and tried to decide the best course of action to take.

First, they tried a couple of informal methods. They got in touch with Carlos Gastel. For his part, Gastel thought the Coles were being pretentious in trying to live in Hancock Park, and he told them so. Why, he didn't even live in a house so fine, he pointed out. But Maria, for one, didn't think much of that argument. Keenly aware of what is proper in a business relationship, she pointed out to Gastel that he was the agent and that he'd *better* not live as they did. Another attorney and member of the Hancock Park Property Owners Association telephoned Cole's road manager, Mort Ruby, to complain, "How would *you* like it if you had to come out of your home and see a Negro walking down the street wearing a big wide hat, a zoot suit, long chain, and yellow shoes?" (Although Maria says that her husband did tend to favor flash in his manner of dressing and that she'd led him to more conservative tastes over the years, there's no evidence that Cole wore zoot suits or otherwise conformed to the stereotype the attorney presented.) At any rate, Ruby was unsympathetic. Although he, too, disapproved of the Coles trying to purchase in Hancock Park, primarily because of the adverse publicity they were inviting, he was determined to support them against racist attacks.

Then the attorney offered to buy back the home from Cole, promising him an additional twenty-five thousand dollars not to purchase the property. Through his own attorney, Cole refused the offer. Marvin Fisher, a music publisher, is reported to have said, "If any of the neighbors want to move out of their homes because of Cole's presence, I'll buy the houses they move out of!"

Thus far, Cole himself had not been approached. At a press conference at the Watkins Hotel he told reporters that he thought he should have been approached directly, since he was the subject of the controversy. He thought he should have the opportunity to meet his future neighbors face-to-face. But the worried Hancock Park Property Owners preferred more indirect methods. As the closing on the property drew near, both the owner of the house and his real estate agent, Ann Winters, received numerous anonymous telephone calls and threats. After anonymous callers told Winters that she would be "driven out of the real estate business" and that she would "meet with a serious automobile accident within a few days," Cole offered her any type of protection she needed, including legal assistance. She chose instead to request help from the Beverly Hills Police Department, which promised her full protection.

On a Monday morning in early August, the various parties closed the deal and Nat King Cole became the owner of a "fourteen room palace." That night Colonel Henry Ganz also requested protection of the Beverly Hills Police Department. For a time guards were stationed around the house, but they were later withdrawn at Ganz's request because they attracted too much attention.

Now the Hancock Park Property Owners Association took formal, legal action. The president of the group presented Cole with an affidavit stating that homes in the section were covered by covenants restricting ownership to Caucasians (and Christian Caucasians) only. This despite the fact that the California courts could no longer enforce these clauses.

Much of the agitation against discrimination in housing at this time, the late 1940s, arose in Hollywood, and where it concerned discrimination against blacks, it was a logical outgrowth of a peculiar federal policy established during the war years, although the framers of that policy had no idea of the indirect repercussions it would have. During the war the hypocrisy of Americans fighting racism and fascism in Europe when racism was endemic in the United States became too evident for most intelligent people to ignore, particularly when many among the American forces were blacks fighting to ensure for foreigners freedoms that they did not themselves enjoy at home. In 1941 the Roosevelt administration had taken tentative steps toward reducing the extent of this hypocrisy. As part of its program to increase employment of blacks in previously restricted fields, especially in defense industries, the administration went a few steps further, informing the major Hollywood studios that the program would benefit from an increase in "a general distribution of important pictures in which Negroes played a major part." Such major all-black films as *Cabin in the Sky* (MGM) and *Stormy Weather* (20th Century Fox) no doubt represented these studios' response to the administration's wishes. Blacks also got more work in "cameos" in otherwise all-white productions. Thus, opportunities in Hollywood began to open up for blacks, and naturally more blacks began to go to Hollywood. They included not just hopeful unknowns but established stars, among them singers like June Richmond, musicians like Benny Carter, and orchestras like Duke Ellington's.

These personalities were accustomed to living in circumstances a few cuts above those of ordinary blacks and were more inclined to take action to achieve a modicum of social justice. In 1948 black actress-activist Frances Williams was the first black to run for the California State Legislature. In terms of housing in Hollywood, they found that suitable accommodations were hard to come by. The middle-class black community in Los Angeles wasn't very large. The majority of homes considered suitable for black stars were, unfortunately, in white neighborhoods. The black stars began to buy these properties, frightened white property owners began to introduce restrictive covenants, and inevitably the question of the legality of these clauses came before the courts. Both Benny Carter and June Richmond brought suit against restrictive covenants. In the meantime, Jews who were barred from property ownership because of such clauses were pursuing the matter as well. The issue of restrictive covenants went all the way to the United States Supreme Court, which declared in early 1948 in *Shelley v. Kraemer* that federal and state courts could not enforce restrictive covenants. While the court did not actually declare the covenants illegal, most people thought it had, and blacks considered the decision a major victory, as did Jews. Nat King Cole believed the law was on his side. He had purchased the home in an

American community, he was an American, and he intended to live in his home.

"It is regrettable that this unfortunate situation has come down," he said. "I am an American citizen, and I feel that I am entitled to the same rights as any other citizen. My wife and I like our home very much and we intend to stay there the same as any other American citizens would."

White realtors and property owners in Los Angeles had been dismayed by the Supreme Court ruling, but they took no concerted action until the Cole case. Cole's purchase of the Hancock Park property seemed to give impetus to an incipient movement to protect the restrictive covenant clauses by constitutional amendment, if necessary. Within days after Cole closed on the house, the president of the Los Angeles Realty Board announced the launching of a campaign to amend the Constitution in this way. The amendment was necessary, said Philip M. Rea, "to protect American family life, stabilize home values, avoid widespread home depreciation, avert racial tensions and to safeguard the rights of families who own comparatively small and modest homes." Rea added that movement by Negroes into once-exclusively Caucasian areas "will necessarily create racial tensions and antagonisms and do much harm to our national social structure." He also proposed that the suggested constitutional amendment be made retroactive, which was no doubt a reference to the Cole case.

Nearly one hundred individual lawsuits by residents of Hancock Park against Cole were threatened, but Cole and Maria went ahead with plans to move into their new home in mid-August. Colonel Ganz moved out on the 14th and headed for India. Shortly after Ganz left the house, someone placed a sign on the front lawn. It read, Nigger Heaven. Although no one ever admitted who put up the sign, the Kansas City *Plaindealer* reported that one of the chief leaders of the anti-Cole crusade was the wife of a prominent businessman, and a resident of South Muirfield Road.

Other organizations of a different persuasion were spurred to act because of the Cole case. James H. Burford, director of the Los Angeles Council of Industrial Organizations (CIO) Political Action Committee issued a statement of support for Cole, pointing out that the CIO "from its initial organization has fought against restrictive covenants." Burford assured Cole that "thousands of members of the CIO and other progressive-minded people in the community will stand behind your fight."

About a month later, the American Civil Liberties Union announced a reward of five hundred dollars for information leading to the arrest, conviction, and imprisonment of anyone found guilty of a misdemeanor or felony against the person or property of a minority race in the process of taking possession of a residence in Southern California. And in late January 1949 the Southern California regional office of the Anti-Defamation League of B'nai B'rith issued a report naming organizations and individuals active in "a campaign of terrorism, vandalism, and discrimination . . . against Southern California families." Among the organizations named in the report were the Los Angeles Realty Board and the Hancock Park Property Owners Association.

Nothing came of the fight to amend the Constitution to legalize restrictive covenants. No one was able to stop the Coles from moving into their new home on August 13, 1948. Their new neighbors did not give up without a parting shot. In the third week of September, a number of gossip columnists, among them Walter Winchell, reported that Cole had been forced to sell the house and had made a fifteen thousand profit guaranteed by the Hancock Park Property Owners Association. Cole had to assure reporters that he had been living in the house for six weeks and had no intention of selling it.

It would be some time before they were able to appreciate the humorous view of their treatment expressed by the writer of the following poem addressed to the editor of the *St. Louis Post-Dispatch* and printed in the August 28, 1948, issue of that paper:

> Nat (King) Cole was a merry young soul,
> And a merry young soul was he.
> He called for a home
> In the white man's zone,
> With a fig for their animosity.
>
> Since the court said no to the whites' tale of woe,
> There was nothing that the whites could say.
> So they tried to buy

At a price sky-high,
But King Cole was there to stay.

It would seem that there ain't any ground for complaint
Which the courts would adjudge as wrong
But I might suggest
That the course next best
Is to sue the King for singing that song.

While I heartily approve of the court's recent move,
And I can't condone restriction's bigotry,
I derive no joy
From the King's "Nature Boy,"
Which I'd like restrained in any key.

Jim Monroe

Nor could most other blacks in Hollywood appreciate the writer's humor. Blacks continued to have trouble buying homes in white areas. Lena Horne and her husband, Lennie Hayton, a Jew, went through considerable harassment when they bought their home in Nichols Canyon in 1949, although by 1951 major hostility had abated. It took courage for these stars to subject themselves to such animosity, but they could at least take heart in the knowledge that the steps of millions of ordinary black people were a little bit lighter for a time after they won that round from bigoted whites.

Maria set about decorating their new home. Because of Nat's busy road schedule and her insistence on accompanying him wherever he went, the entire job wasn't finished until just before they celebrated their first anniversary. But in Maria's opinion the final product was worth the wait. The house was a showcase. Tom Douglas, a noted Hollywood decorator, oversaw the job, with considerable help from Maria, who, Nat said some years later, put her "personal stamp on it." One wall of the 33- by 16-foot living room featured a 13-foot-long floor-to-ceiling mirror; and a 26-foot-long string-cotton rug covered the floor. The room sported an 8-foot custom-built sofa and four armchairs upholstered in a silk print of white background with a tropical pattern in green and chartreuse. The shades of the six 30-inch-high column lamps were white silk trimmed in salmon. The master bedroom upstairs was done in blue and pink. The king-size bed had a 5- by 8-foot headstand upholstered in pink antique satin with white trim. Behind it, pink shirred silk topped by a pink custom-made cornice created a curtained-window effect. On the blue walls at either side of the bed was a hand-painted vine-and-blossom design. The ceiling was also blue. A chair and a chaise lounge near the bed were upholstered in pink-and-white–striped fabric. The master bedroom also featured a sitting area centered around a white fireplace; the chairs were covered in white satin with pink trim. Above the fireplace was a shoulder-length portrait of Maria Cole. A pool for the rear of the house was still in the planning stages when Maria invited *Ebony* to do a picture spread on the Coles' mansion.

At his wife's urging, Nat Cole converted to the Episcopal Church. His family were infrequent visitors to the house on South Muirfield Road, except for Eddie, who visited from time to time. No zoot-suited musicians walked the streets of the neighborhood; there were no wild parties, and according to Geri Branton Nat practiced even his piano playing elsewhere. The Coles were models of propriety, and even their most vigilant neighbors could find nothing in their behavior cause for complaint. Eventually the furor over their having broken the Hancock Park housing barrier died down. The worst fears of the older residents were not realized; Hancock Park remains largely white to this day. "It is *the* posh area, the last WASP enclave," says Geri Branton. "There are about two Jewish and three black families there. After Nat died and Maria moved back East, a black woman, Zelma Stinnis, bought their house; it's interesting that a white person didn't buy it." By then, Hancock Park residents no longer felt any urgency to reclaim the house from blacks.

Says Kelly Cole, whom the Coles adopted in 1959, "By [the time I came along] we were an old respected family. Natalie was born in 1950, and she can't remember any trouble. She remembers back to 1953 or 1954. Basically, that was because of my mother's steadying influence. She's such a lady, and the house was done so nicely, and we were pretty well-behaved kids. Everyone just got used to it. In fact, we were much better behaved than most of the other kids on the block. I had three friends—two brothers and this other guy named Gregory—and I got along real well with them until they started getting wild. My mother, being as conservative as she is, cut the relationship off when I was eleven."

Throughout the time he was fighting to "live like an artist," as Cole put it, he continued to be an artist. The July 14, 1948, issue of *Down Beat* paid tribute to him in that regard when they ran a column devoted to his musicianship. It read in part, "In an effort to capture the individual traits that characterize Cole's piano styling, this column asked him to provide a spontaneously conceived rendition based on a simple melody to be furnished just prior to the time for recording the example. Nat played through the original melody once, paused for a few minutes reflection, and then 'took off' into the accompanying artistic improvisation that clearly indicates the ability and resourcefulness which are responsible for his tremendous and deserved success."

The column, written by Sharon A. Pease, went on to set forth the harmonic sequence of the original and to outline what Nat did with the material. For example: "The standard fundamental harmony for such codettas, in this key, is tonic, C followed by the sequence C-7, A-7, D-7, G-7, and finally the delayed tonic close. Nat uses a sequence of C-7, A-7 with augmented fifth and added dissonant tone (lowered third), D-minor-7, G-7, plus the sixth, followed by the delayed tonic with added sixth and ninth." There is more technical musical comment but those who wish to read all of that can get it from the library.

The article concluded, "The true differences between individuals become more apparent in the actual performance. It is in this final step that gifted musicians are able to display those individual characteristics that set them apart. Outstanding among Nat's performance attributes are the creation of a rhythmic pulse so dominant that it is recreated in the feelings of the listener and the technical precision that makes all similar rhythms uniformally (sic) accurate: i.e., A dotted eighth on the second count is exactly the same length as a dotted eighth on the first count and the last in a group of sixteenths is exactly the same length as all similar values in the passage."

The King Cole Trio met all its club commitments during the time of the Hancock Park furor and promoted the records that Capitol issued practically on a monthly basis. (The Petrillo ban was still in effect, and all these tunes had been recorded before January 1, 1948. "We have enough recordings made ahead to last for five years," Cole announced.) In addition to an album containing such songs as "I'm in the Mood for Love" and "I Know That You Know," Capitol issued a three-record album called *King Cole for Kids* containing nursery rhymes and other children's favorites. A well-received single paired "Little Girl" and "Baby, Baby All the Time." Wrote a reviewer for the Portland, Oregon, *Journal,* "One of Mr. Cole's greatest gifts is his ability to say 'Baby.'" Also, on "Baby, Baby All the Time," critics praised the fine interplay of Cole's piano and Ashby's guitar.

As agreed, after leaving Ciro's, they played the Million Dollar Theater for a week, and from their performing one never would have guessed that Cole was having serious personal problems. Wrote Marie Nesmer in the *Los Angeles News,* "Probably one reason why [the trio has] excelled is because they not only play rhythm, but they think and feel it. You can't escape a sincerity in Cole's voice either, and as many times as I have heard him sing he hasn't given a bad performance." Ironically, Benny Carter, who'd had his own problems with restrictive covenants, was on the same bill with his orchestra. Meanwhile, Joe Comfort was having problems of his own, having become embroiled in a complicated divorce suit.

The night after they ended their stint at the Million Dollar Theater, the trio opened at Lloyd Johnson's Klub Kona. From there they traveled to Portland, Oregon, for a concert, then to Vancouver, British Columbia, to play the Palomar Club for two weeks. Back in California, at the County Bowl, they performed their first concert outdoors. Although Cole found he had a little trouble warming up his fingers, he thought playing outdoors was "quite an experience." According to the reviewer for the *Santa Barbara News Press,* the outdoor conditions "didn't seem to cramp their easy-going style at all." Once again, Irving Ashby came in for special praise: "Ashby, the guitar man, scored a hit with his own composition 'Allegro Suite.' His fingering of the instrument in unison with Cole is uncanny." Appearing with them on the program was a comparative newcomer, a composer-arranger with MGM and a Victor recording artist named André Previn.

The trio's concert style was as polished as their club act. Wrote a reviewer for the *Portland Oregonian,* "They use stage lights for phantasia effects that make the three men on the stage seem like a whole orchestra at times. Cole and his wing men kick in with comic didoes, little games of handies here and there that tend to keep the customers from straining their bifocals looking for faults and flats. In fact, the boys got almost as many chuckles as they did kudos."

Back in L.A. they moved into the Red Feather Club, corner of Manchester and Figueroa, for four weeks. Sir Charles and Lady Mendl (Elsie de Wolfe) and a group of Beverly Hills friends chartered a plane and flew down for the opening. Less than two weeks later the trio began shooting on Columbia's film musical *Make Believe Ballroom,* starring the originator of the radio disc jockey program by that name, Al Jarvis. They were a specialty act in the film, along with Charlie Barnett, Peewee Hunt, Gene Krupa, Kay Starr, Jimmy Dorsey and his orchestra, Frankie Laine, and a number of others.

Just about the time the trio began filming at Columbia, they became embroiled in a controversy with the management of the Red Feather. Shortly before they opened at the club, owners Paul Shipton and Andy Andrews concluded a deal with KTLA-TV for a series of Monday night telecasts (the first "remote control" television broadcasts from a nightclub in Southern California), featuring the headliners at the club, who would be paid straight union scale, or $9.20 per half hour, for their television services. The series was inaugurated the week before the Cole Trio opened and deemed a success, and both the owners of the Red Feather and the KTLA-TV people looked forward to televising Cole and his combo. They neglected to check with Cole and Carlos Gastel, however, and had put nothing into the trio's contract about the telecasts.

At 3 P.M. on the afternoon before opening night, Gastel informed Shipton and Andrews that the King Cole Trio would not accept straight union scale. In addition, Gastel said, the trio's radio contract barred them from appearing on television.

Shipton and Andrews had to hustle to find a replacement for the half hour during which the trio was to have been televised. Dick Petersen (and His Music of Audible Illusion), the first group formed in L.A. specifically for television, was happy to fill in. For the balance of the time the trio performed at the Red Feather, the club's owners had to find fill-in acts for the Monday night video broadcasts. Naturally, this rankled with them, since they felt that the $3,500 a week they were paying the trio was a sufficiently hefty sum. Although Cole wasn't the only performer to refuse to be televised—Kenny Pierce also did not appear, as the Red Feather would have had to pay him a week's salary just for the television stint, as per American Guild of Variety Artists (AGVA) ruling—his refusal almost caused KTLA-TV to drop the project altogether. From then on, relations between the trio and the management of the Red Feather were strained at best.

On Friday, October 1, following their regularly scheduled show, the trio pulled out of the Red Feather. Reportedly, the move came at the insistence of Ed Bailey, president of Local 767 of the Negro Musicians Union, and Carlos Gastel, who cited "intolerable working conditions." The Red Feather owners and the agent apparently had no hard feelings, for another of Gastel's acts, the Alice Hall Trio, replaced the Cole group for the remaining day of its original contract. But rancor between the Red Feather and the Cole Trio continued. The club had payment stopped on checks amounting to $1,135, covering the trio's last three days of work, claiming that members of Cole's crew had left tabs amounting to about $300.

On the same day that the Cole Trio pulled out of the Red Feather, Maria and a friend were robbed on a Hollywood street. The newspapers identified the friend as Mrs. Gerry Nicholas, but it was Geri Nicholas, wife of Fayard Nicholas of the Nicholas Brothers (and later Geri Branton). They had stopped at Schwab's drugstore. "Maria was wearing *all* of her jewelry, and that must have attracted him," says Geri Branton. "I remember that a young, Nazi-looking chap brushed past us." When the two women returned to Branton's car, the man was hiding on the floor of the back seat. "When we got into the car, he put a gun to the back of my head and demanded money. We gave him about eighty dollars. He got out of the car at Sunset and Vine and disappeared in the crowd." Ironically, he took none of the jewelry the women were wearing. While Maria and Geri considered themselves lucky not to have been harmed and to have kept their jewelry, it was, for Maria and for her husband, one more aggravation in a very trying time.

The King Cole Trio moved into Billy Berg's on October 4 for a four-week stint, participated in a star-studded benefit for the bombed Hadassah Hospital in Israel (Lucille Ball, Desi Arnaz, Keenan Wynn, Danny Kaye, Al Jarvis, Chico Marx, John Garfield, and Carmen Miranda were among the other entertainers who appeared) on October 14, and on October 28 staged a "farewell concert" at the Avodon Ballroom. Cole rented the ballroom and hired an orchestra for the occasion, which was simply the group's last appearance in Southern California before going on an Eastern tour. While the occasion did not seem to warrant a "farewell concert," perhaps it was Cole's way of showing that he was undeterred, personally and professionally, by the problems he was having.

The fast-paced schedule of that Eastern tour was as follows:

Palace, Youngstown, Ohio, November 1 (3 days)
Club Tijuana, Cleveland, week of November 4
Keith Theater, Dayton, week of November 11
Rivoli Theater, Toledo, 4 days
Palace, Columbus, 3 days
Albee, Cincinnati, week of November 25
Showboat, Milwaukee, week of December 2
Oriental, Chicago, weeks of December 9 and 16

At the Tijuana in Cleveland, the trio broke its own attendance record. At the Showboat in Milwaukee, working under a deal that provided for $3,500 against 60 percent of the gross, they set a new attendance record and pocketed as their share $11,200. At the Oriental in Chicago, they played for a flat $5,000 per week.

That was big money in those days, and for Cole these sums were exclusive of record royalty income. He'd enjoyed consistent recording successes that year, though none of his records had equaled the popularity of "Nature Boy." Had Eden Ahbez presented him with another song like "Nature Boy," he couldn't have recorded it, for the Petrillo ban was still in effect. People often asked Cole about Ahbez. In late August 1948 Cole said, "He's still living the same way (in a sleeping bag) near Los Angeles and writing songs. As soon as the recording ban is lifted and he can get some songs recorded, he might produce another 'Nature Boy.' He's sung a couple more for me. They're pretty good, but you never know what is going to be great."

On another occasion, he said, "You know, Eden Ahbez is a funny guy. He's hard to talk to. He's always spouting philosophy and biblical talk. I know a lot of people thought [the reports in the media were] a lot of bunk, a publicity stunt, but take it from me, every word of it is true.... He sure is a funny guy."

Although Cole's recordings released in the latter part of 1948 weren't blockbusters like "Nature Boy," they were nevertheless good music. His rendition of "Put 'Em in a Box, Tie 'Em with a Ribbon and Throw 'Em in the Deep Blue Sea," from Warner's *Romance on the High Seas* was considered by many to be better than other versions, including Eddy Howard's and Doris Day's. His "A Woman Always Understands"/"Lillette" received good reviews. "Don't Blame Me"/"I've Got a Way with Women" sold well, too. The album, *King Cole for Kids,* was among the top fifteen best-selling children's records for 1948, and by early January 1949 *King Cole—Vol. No. 3* was among the top five best-selling albums. Capitol had planned well for the year-long Petrillo ban. The King Cole Trio still had nearly forty unreleased sides.

But for all the money he was making on concert tours and long-term club bookings and record royalties, Cole had big expenses that put a crimp in his profits. Crew, managers, publicists, valets, and secretaries had to be paid. Forty percent of his gross earnings went to booking and personal managing—20 percent to General Artists' Corporation, Carlos Gastel's agency, alone. He paid four people as press agents—Don Haines and Gene Howard on the West Coast, Virginia Wicks on the East Coast, and Billy Rowe of the *Pittsburgh Courier* to handle the Negro press. He had two business managers, William De Haas and George Stuart, and a road manager, Mort Ruby. Then there was the salary of his secretary-valet, Johnny Hopkins. Traveling cost a lot. Booked for eighty-eight one-night stands in 1948, the trio averaged $250 a night just in tips to bellhops, elevator operators, stagehands, taxi drivers, laundry and tailor services. Cole wasn't one to forget the little people, the people who, if treated right, would treat him right. While he was generous by nature and by nature inclined to remember where he had come from, he was also, as his son, Kelly, says, shrewd—traveling on the road was hard, but it could be a little bit easier if you had people like bellhops and elevator operators on your side. Clothes were another major budget item—Cole wore out ten $175 suits a year. An additional personal expense was the salary for C. W. Shaw, caretaker of the house in Hancock Park. Since Maria traveled with him, Cole had to have someone to look after his hard-won home, and on November 18 Shaw was on the premises to report to the police that a window in the house had been broken by a blunt pellet, probably from an air gun, as a car whizzed by.

When asked about his expenses, Cole didn't think to mention income taxes. Perhaps he believed that the business managers to whom he paid substantial salaries were taking care of such things. He certainly didn't have the time or the inclination to think about them as 1948 drew to a close and he and his trio and his wife of less than a year traveled around the Midwest and then on to the East Coast.

They spent Christmas in New York, the trio appearing at the Annual Breakfast Show and Dance at the Renaissance Ballroom on December 24, taking a breather on Christmas Day. The Coles kept an apartment there, and Maria shopped and got in touch with friends. They went to Washington, D.C., for a dance and three-nightclub date, then returned to New York for New Year's. During the holiday week, *Cash Box* announced that the King Cole Trio had been voted "outstandingly" the best small instrumental group of 1948 and second in the best male vocal combination category. That same week the *Down Beat* poll results showed the King Cole Trio holding second place behind Joe Ventura in the small group instrumental combo category. Having placed second in *Billboard*'s annual college poll in both small instrumental group and small vocal group sections in 1947, they captured the number one spot in both sections in 1948, carrying off twice as many votes as their nearest rivals (the Benny Goodman Sextet in the small band category, which had placed first in 1947, had been outpaced by both the King Cole Trio and the Suns, Victor artists whose hit was "Twilight Time"). In addition, Cole himself won the poll as number one vocalist over Perry Como and Frankie Laine. Modestly, Cole pointed out that neither Bing Crosby nor Frank Sinatra was competing and said, "I can't sing. It's just that I have a style and I put it across." The trio also won the *Metronome* best small band designation for the third year in a row.

Considering that Cole was working with two new sidemen during 1948 and considering that he'd received a lot of adverse publicity that year over his purchase of the Hancock Park house, his winning so many awards is a testament both to his own unwavering talent and to his ability to choose musicians who could complement it. It is a testament as well to the fact that at least where their music was concerned, a substantial number of Americans were able to put racial considerations aside.

6

Trio to Quartet

COLE'S sidemen took a couple of days off as the new year dawned, but he remained at the piano. He accompanied his wife at a brief engagement in Boston, where at the Hi-Hat, Maria returned to the stage to sing "Don't Blame Me for Falling in Love with You." A native of Boston, she felt comfortable being onstage there and realized how much she had missed performing. Cole, however, was adamantly against her resuming her career. There was room for only one career in the Cole family. If Cole had had his way, the family would have been composed of more than two, but Maria wasn't ready to have children. She didn't want the responsibility just yet. If she could not get her husband to agree to a resumption of her career, then at least she would be as close to the show business life as possible, traveling with the trio. She enjoyed appearing in public as Mrs. Nat King Cole. Whenever he opened at a club, she wore a tiara, knowing that reporters would pick up on the symbolism and write about her as Nat's "Queen."

Then, too, she had an investment to protect in her husband; and her determination to be with him at all costs would persist even after they did have children.

After the brief trip to Boston, Cole and his two sidemen reunited for a weekend at the State Theater in Hartford, Connecticut. From there they went to Philadelphia for a week-long stint at Frank Palumbo's Click, then to Pittsburgh for a week at the Copa Club, where they broke the profit and attendance record previously set by Frankie Laine.

Before the opening, the Copa's management asked Carlos Gastel if Cole would be willing to do a Saturday matinee at no extra fee. Reportedly Gastel said no, that it was not in the contract. Yet when Cole arrived at the club, unaware of the exchange between management and manager, he suggested that the trio do the very same extra show that the Copa people had wanted. Wrote Harold V. Cohen of the *Pittsburgh Post-Gazette,* who reported the story, "Things like that are what make big people in show business even bigger people."

From Pittsburgh they went to Chicago and the Blue Note for three weeks. There, a reviewer noted, "Nature Boy" was not in the group's repertoire. "Unless request-pressured, Nat seems to avoid the grass-skirt ballad... But Cole still flings around 'Sweet Lorraine.'" Winding up their stay at the Blue Note on February 13, they had three days to rest up and prepare for their first combined tour with a white group, Woody Herman's Band.

Woodrow Charles Herman and his all-white big band, which he fondly called his Herd, had made a name for themselves as a swing group. During the mid-1940s, however, Herman changed the style of his music, allowing greater freedom of improvisation and incorporating the musical developments of bebop into his arrangements. Before that time, bebop had been primarily the province of small combos, most notably Dizzy Gillespie's. Herman's was the first prominent big band to incorporate bebop elements into its music. With the help of arranger Ralph Burns, the Herman Herd made two important recordings in 1947 and 1948: "Four Brothers" and "Early Autumn." More harmonically aggressive than their earlier recordings and containing adaptations of the bebop unison riff, these tunes retained the traditional brass solos. Outstanding on both discs were the tenor solos of Stan Getz that, according to Frank Tirro in

Jazz: A History, were "the beginnings of a new school in jazz, the 'cool school,' which would soon separate itself from the parent bebop."

Herman and his band were also managed by Carlos Gastel, who'd put the combined tour together; Herman and Cole knew each other well. Whether out of respect for Herman or out of respect for the musical marketplace or whether, as he explained, "As a trio we'd gone as far as we could—We'd done about everything except imitations," Cole decided to introduce some bebop into the style of the King Cole Trio for the combined tour. To play conga and bongo drums, he hired Jack Costanzo, who'd been featured with Stan Kenton's orchestra playing the bongo drums, an instrument as yet so unfamiliar to the lay public that newspaper writers felt constrained to explain that they were "two small drums with a light, sharp tone, that are played with the fingers and the palm of the hand and are standard equipment in Latin American bands. Modern musicians have leaned more and more toward Latin American rhythms in recent years." In fact, the headline writer for the *California Eagle* was so unfamiliar with the instrument that the paper's February 17, 1949, article about the addition of bongo player Constanzo read "Banjo Player Added to King Cole Trio."

Some newspapers reported that Cole's new sideman was named Vidal. Joe Comfort explains, "Carlos Vidal was the one that Nat really thought he was getting. Vidal used to play with Stan Kenton. Instead, he got Jack Costanzo." Constanzo also played with Stan Kenton and joined the Cole Trio directly from the Kenton orchestra. Says Irving Ashby, "When Dizzy Gillespie came up here from Brazil with Charo and a conga drum in his orchestra, Stan Kenton decided he'd better get a conga drum, too. He didn't want to be outdone. He hired Jack Costanzo. Jack could handle it all—congas, tymbales, etc.—and so Stan Kenton thought he would come out ahead by hiring just one guy. But Kenton didn't realize that in African rhythms there's no one guy who can play all the instruments simultaneously. In that respect, Stan Kenton defeated his purpose. When Stan found out that he'd have to hire two or three more guys to get the sound that Gillespie was getting, Jack was sort of assigned to certain parts of the arrangement. That didn't work out, and when Stan let him go Nat hired him. . . . Maybe Carlos Gastel had something to do with it, because he managed Stan Kenton, too."

Costanzo was a Chicagoan who had started out as a dancer. In fact, he was a sixteen-year-old dance instructor at a Chicago club when he became fascinated with the bongo drum in the club's rhumba band. With his wife-to-be, Marguerite Myers, a fellow dance teacher who used the name Marda professionally, he formed a dance team, Costanzo and Marda, and since the rhumba was one of their specialties, he continued to be exposed to the exotic drums. At length, he gave up dancing for drumming and was with Rene Touzet's rhumba band when Stan Kenton first heard him.

Neither Ashby nor Comfort was consulted about the hiring of a drummer. "Nat did things on his own," says Ashby. "The only consultation I can imagine he took—or at least that was obvious he took—was from Carlos Gastel. He'd occasionally listen to songwriters and people in the A & R [Artists and Repertory] department, but they never had any real decision-making power. Maria and Carlos were the ones, and Carlos, I think, gritted his teeth every time he saw Maria coming."

Press reports on Cole's hiring of Costanzo, however, indicate that Capitol Records executives had some input into Cole's decisions. One executive was quoted as saying, "The trio seemed to be too much of the same thing." A look at the recordings made by Cole and the trio in 1949 seems to indicate a concerted effort toward newness, with a number of recordings featuring vocal groups and orchestras. Cole himself, however, did speak of the trio needing more depth and a broader scope: "The change gives us that progressive feeling. A lot of ideas have come out already. We're going to be able to do much more. Jack relaxes the guys. A lot of the tension the bass and I used to feel is gone now because the bongo and conga drums give the rhythm we were supposed to give. That leaves us free to do much more."

Still, it was a hard adjustment. The press and the public had a difficult time with the idea of a fourth member of the "trio." Even the newspapers that reported, correctly, that Jack Costanzo not Vidal was joining the Cole group had trouble with his name, which was variously reported as Costonzo, Costanza, and Castany. "Castany" was Cole's nickname for his newest sideman.

For Ashby and Comfort, the adjustment was considerably more difficult. Costanzo was white, but they didn't mind that so much. What they say they minded most was the fact that Constanzo's drums just didn't fit. "He was the beginning of the end of my happiness with the King Cole Trio," says Ashby. "Can you imagine conga drums on 'Sweet Lorraine?' That just turned my stomach—ker-plak, ker-plak, ker-plak. But what could I say? I wasn't paying him. I just did the job."

Says Comfort, "I didn't like it at all. And Irving didn't like it. We both didn't like it because it just didn't fit. A conga drum with a bass and guitar and piano—it's too lopey—clack-a-lack-a lack-a lack. If you play 'Sweet Lorraine' with a guy playing a conga drum, it would sound like something loping, like a horse clopping his feet."

Ashby and Comfort soon felt they had reason to dislike Costanzo for more than his music. "Jack was always with Marie discussing the latest evening gowns and jewelry," says Ashby. "We'd be on the train riding someplace and instead of being with us, talking or playing cards with the guys or having a sip or something, he'd be sitting with the boss's wife yakking about the latest things from the perfume world. So you can imagine what kind of an impression he made on us."

The arrival of Jack Costanzo signaled a basic change in the Cole group that some suggest was what Maria had in mind all along: With the addition of Costanzo, the trio was no longer a trio but a quartet. The group's billing was changed from the King Cole Trio to Nat Cole and His Trio. Irving Ashby remembers that their wardrobe underwent a change as well. "We all used to wear the same clothes—if we were wearing blue, we all wore it. We had our suits made by Sy Deveaux in L.A. and other big tailors. When Costanzo came on the scene, he was the odd man." It was not long afterward that Nat Cole became that odd man or, in his case, the featured man. When the trio wore dark blue, Cole wore light grey. The separation of the man from his men continued.

There was also a change in road managers at that time. Mort Ruby was joined by Carl Carruthers. Carruthers, who had been a dining car waiter on the Pennsylvania Railroad, recalls his first meeting with Nat: "I met him when I was hanging out in a club—the Persian Room at some hotel in Chicago," says Carruthers. "After he finished his show at the Blue Note, he would come down and catch the last show at the Persian Room. I saw him one night—he had on a beautiful hat and coat and I admired them. We got into a conversation. Next thing I knew, I was signed up to go on tour with him and Woody Herman. I did transportation, lights, sound, driving. Baldwin Tabares, Irving Ashby's brother-in-law, took care of costumes. He also did some advance hotel reservations. His name didn't sound black, and it was easier to get them confirmed."

Shuffled around and reassembled, the group now billed as Nat Cole and His Trio joined up with Woody Herman and His Herd to open their joint concert tour in Champaign, Illinois. Traveling as an integrated group didn't present much of a problem, Ashby remembers, because the blacks usually stayed in private homes: "They were all competing with one another to get Nat and Marie to stay in their homes." Gastel had worked out a deal calling for either a straight 70 percent of each night's gross or a $3,000-per-night guarantee against 50 percent of the take. The performers left Champaign with $6,800, or 70 percent.

They had a couple of days before their next concert, so they went to Chicago. There Cole and Herman were the only two non-family members invited to the wedding of Mel Tormé, author of Cole's hit "The Christmas Song," and Florence Gertrude Tockstein, a Hollywood starlet who had also gone by the names Candy Toxton, Brooke Chase, Linda Howard, and Susan Perry. The twenty-three-year-old Tormé was already nicknamed "The Velvet Fog." After the wedding his bride gave up her movie career, even though the movie in which she had her first big role—as Humphrey Bogart's wife in *Knock on Any Door*—had yet to be released.

The next stop on the Cole-Herman tour was Ames, Iowa. All had planned to drive there from Chicago, but Herman decided the roads were too bad. He flew from Chicago to Des Moines, then took a taxi from Des Moines to Ames. The Cole group decided to drive in spite of the poor road conditions.

There were eight people in the rented car—Cole, his trio, Maria, his road managers, Ruby and Carruthers, and his program man, Bill Kalman. Outside Peoria, Illinois, where a very young Richard Pryor was just discovering that he could make people laugh, the car skidded on an icy road and turned over in a ditch. Although the car was practically demolished, miraculously no one was hurt in the crash. Joe Comfort, whose attorney had just succeeded in persuading his former wife to accept a flat one thousand dollars as a divorce settlement, was especially aware of the potential irony had the crash been fatal to him. Cole sprained his ankle extricating himself from the overturned car; but his was the only injury. They managed to hitch a ride on a bakery truck to police headquarters; then, having reported the accident, they rented another car for the rest of the trip to Ames.

At the University of Iowa, as at the University of Illinois in Champaign, King Cole and His Trio opened the program with such selections as "Little Girl" and "Top Hat Bop." Costanzo was featured on "Rhumba Azul," Joe Comfort on "Down Front." "Baby I Need You," "Sweet Lorraine," "Body and Soul," and "Honeysuckle Rose" were well received by the type of audience that had cast so many votes for Cole and his group in the annual *Billboard* polls. They demanded encores of "Straighten Up and Fly Right" and "Nature Boy."

Then Woody Herman and the Herd played their bebop selections, punctuated by songs by Herman and the band's singer, Mary Ann McCall. For the grand finale, Woody and His Herd and Cole and His Trio combined their talents in a jazz arrangement of "How High the Moon."

"WHAKCS" were put on sale at the Memorial Union Grill in Ames. An acronym for a Woody Herman and King Cole Special Sundae, the concoction was ice cream rolled in macaroons, covered with caramel and chocolate sauces and topped with a cherry.

The Cole and Herman show performed next at Carnegie Hall, sharing the bill with Harry Belafonte, whom the *New York Mirror* called the "singing discovery at The Royal Roost." Then they played Town Hall in Philadelphia, an especially pleasurable gig for Herman's singer, Mary Ann McCall, for whom Philadelphia was home. At each of the fourteen performances, the tour was so well received and so lucrative (the two combos split forty-eight thousand in profits) that in mid-March they announced a second combined tour, this time on the West Coast, to begin in August.

Cole and his group returned to their individual schedule. In Philadelphia they played the Paramount for a week, sharing the bill with Elliot Lawrence and his orchestra, impressionist Larry Storch, and comedy dancers Helen and Howard. The film attractions at the Paramount were *Moonrise,* starring Dane Clark, Gail Russell, and Ethel Barrymore, and

Alias Nick Beal, starring Ray Milland. After that they appeared in New York at a Spring Bock Festival sponsored by the New York Brewers' Board of Trade and the New Jersey Brewers' Association. It was the first time in seven years that bock beer (made from burnt malt and brewed and aged twice as long as regular beer) had been available in large quantities, for its production had been curtailed during the war to save materials. The festival, which benefited the American Red Cross, attracted such crowds that extra police had to be called out. The midway provided continuous music from, in addition to King Cole and His Trio, the bands of Skitch Henderson and Cab Calloway and Karl Weiss's Bavarian Peasant Band. A special exhibition fight featuring Sugar Ray Robinson and refereed by Ray Bolger was interrupted when Robinson accidentally hit Bolger in the nose. The dancing comedian said the injury would not keep him out of his current Broadway hit, *Where's Charley?*

As always, there were new records to push at these performances. Among them was "No Moon at All"/"It Only Happens Once." While "No Moon at All," written by Redd Evans and Dave Mann, was the major side, Sherm Feller of the *Boston American* gave equal space to "It Only Happens Once," which Frankie Laine had written. Said Feller, "I also enjoyed [Nat's] pianistics on the platter. Nat plays very delicately, yet gets some pretty figures into this side."

Fans of Cole's piano playing were treated to an entire album that spring. *King Cole at the Piano* was just what the title promised—Nat King Cole with rhythm accompaniment but without vocals. The album included "Cole Capers," "These Foolish Things," "Three Little Words," "I'll Never Be the Same," "How High the Moon," and "Blues in My Shower," among other selections. While some critics praised it—Walter Kerr in the *New York World Telegram* wrote, "When Nat (King) Cole sits down at the piano, you can be sure sparkling piano will be the order of the day"—others found something missing. Wrote Bruno David Ussher in the *San Diego Tribune Sun,* "It is difficult to warm up about 'King Cole' and his new soliloquies. Cole's flitting piano style is preferable to Shearings'. His accents are more pertinent and 'loser' [sic] in a teasing manner. . . . An entire album of this type of rambling however proves again that there is a lack of ideas." And Louis Green of the *San Francisco People's World* called Cole a "baffling pianist. He frequently displays some really ingenious—but empty—gymnastics, while, other times, he hits the bell on something real and different."

Purely instrumental albums—particularly ones that were basically a man at a piano—were not very commercial. One suspects that Cole felt the need to remind people, and perhaps even himself, that he was a musician first and foremost. Already people were beginning to think of him as a singer backed up by a small combo. Not that he intended to give up singing.

Around March 1949 he decided to take his singing to an area of the country he had previously avoided: the South. This wasn't an easy decision for Cole, for he knew that he and his group would face problems traveling and obtaining accommodations that would be much worse and more numerous than those they regularly experienced in the North and West.

In April 1949 Cole and his group were in Pittsburgh, playing at Bill Green's, and he was refused registration at one of the city's finest hotels. He answered that discrimination by bringing a twenty-five thousand dollar suit against the California firm that ran the hotel. Playing in Las Vegas was no picnic for them either, despite Cole's insistence in 1946 that he would not play there again under segregated conditions. Joe Comfort remembers that as blacks, they were subjected to plenty of discrimination: "We had to stay in the back, couldn't go out front and gamble at the tables or anything. It was at the Thunderbird, and we were there about two weeks. We stayed across the tracks, over in some wooden units. There were some other blacks there—Bunny Briggs, a tap dancer, others. After the show we would go back over to Dustville. We could gamble there; the Chinese had places where you could play poker and dice. I remember Nat saying that he wasn't going back there if we had to stay in the back like that. We didn't go back, but after I left he did."

If they experienced that kind of treatment in Pittsburgh and Las Vegas, no wonder Cole had avoided performing below the Mason-Dixon Line. In the South, the problems would be much more serious than finding a place to gamble or being barred from a white hotel. In the South, a black would not presume even to try.

A small crack in the wall of Southern segregation had begun to open, however. In late 1948 the Monte Carlo in Miami Beach had instituted what columnist Irv Kupcinet called a "revolutionary policy" by bringing in black entertainers. No black entertainers had ever been permitted to work in a white club in the South before. The first black attraction, the Ink Spots, had, according to Kupcinet, "saved [the club] from a lot of red ink spots." Bill Bojangles Robinson had proved to be a major attraction, too. "Now," wrote Kupcinet, "other night spots here are dickering for such stars as Lena Horne, Cab Calloway and the King Cole Trio." The Clover Club quickly followed the Monte Carlo's lead, signing Cab Calloway. They, too, approached Carlos Gastel. Although no agreement was immediately reached with either Miami Beach club, Cole did decide that conditions in the South might have changed enough to permit him to take his music to Dixie. The late May to early July schedule that was arranged would take the group to thirty cities in the bastion of white supremacy.

Theater and club owners had some strict requirements. In most cities Cole and his group would have to perform before segregated audiences—for blacks or for whites but not for mixed audiences. Cole agreed to that restriction. Three cities—Shreveport, Louisiana; Little Rock, Arkansas; and Montgomery, Alabama (his hometown)—barred an integrated act, and Cole had to agree not to include Jack Costanzo in his combo while playing those towns. "They wouldn't even let Jack come to town on the bus with us," says Irving Ashby. "They'd stop us outside the city limits and say he couldn't ride into town with us. They'd take him off, in fact. He'd stay at a white place in town, and the next day, when we left, he would be brought to the bus." In effect, then, in these cities Costanzo was paid to do nothing; but neither Ashby nor Comfort resented this. The Cole group still hung together in a pinch. "The way the trio was, no one cared about that stuff," says Ashby. "The whole idea was so repulsive in the first place we would have given up our salaries; and I imagine Nat would have paid [Costanzo] four or five times his salary just to have him, because he was part of us."

For his part, Cole, through Gastel, had secured a guarantee of 60 percent of gross against $1,500 to $2,500 for each one-night stand and $55,000 overall, softening somewhat the other undignified terms of his contracts.

In general, the tour was more pleasant than Cole had expected. The group had arranged for accommodations in advance, and there were no unhappy surprises such as Cole himself had experienced in Pittsburgh. Maria stayed in New York during most of the tour. "She didn't want to deal with that [segregation]," says Comfort. "Her stomping ground was New York." Some of the mundane experiences of traveling through a segregated land were funny even at the time, not just in retrospect.

"We traveled by bus," says Joe Comfort. "It was painted red, white, and blue and had our name on the side. We had a big old fat [white] bus driver—Barney—nice guy—weighed about 320 pounds. I think he was from Chicago." Comfort, who was born and raised in Watts, had been stationed in Alabama during the war. He remembered the experience of segregation then as dehumanizing: "Never before had I felt that bad." But several years later, traveling with King Cole, Comfort was as ill-prepared for segregation as he had been at boot camp—particularly when he encountered it immediately on waking.

"The bus stopped at one of those truck stops," he recalls. "I was asleep, and when I woke up all the guys were off the bus. So I went in the front door, not even thinking. There was a long counter, and people were sitting there eating. There was a door to the back, and I saw Nat and Irving and the others standing at the back door, and I thought they were waiting to go to the bathroom. So I stayed out in front and ordered a ham sandwich and a Coke to go. I get back on the bus, and they say, 'Man, what are you doing? You're going to get us put in jail! You're supposed to go to the back!'

"The same thing happened another time. I was asleep, and I don't know why Nat and Irving didn't say anything to me, because when I was going in the door of the place, they were coming out. Barney was sitting at the counter, and there wasn't anybody else in there, so I went and sat by Barney. The waitress says, 'I'm sorry, we don't serve colored here.' I said, 'Well, I don't blame you. Will you please give me a ham sandwich and a cup of coffee.' Barney starts laughing and his belly is up against the counter and the whole counter starts shaking. I was so mad I didn't give a damn. She brought it, and I sat there and ate it."

Comfort remembers riding a ferry in Norfolk, Virginia, and seeing

"Colored and White drinking fountains, Colored and White toilets," but they had known to expect these things in the South and had prepared for them as best they could.

The major unpleasantness occurred in Memphis toward the end of the tour. In the third week of June, the municipal censorship board refused to allow Jack Costanzo to play a concert at the W. C. Handy Theater, a blacks-only film theater located in the heart of the Beale Street sector and named after the famous blues composer. It was the only occasion in which a municipality itself barred a mixed group from performing. In the cases of the three other cities, theater or club owners had asked that Costanzo not appear, although local police had enforced the requests.

Over all, Cole considered the tour a success. He and his group emerged relatively unscathed and with a respectable sum of money in their pockets—$3,270 for one night in Atlanta, $2,900 for one night in Chattanooga—close to $100,000 for forty-two dates. And in later years Cole would have another reason to look back upon that tour with some fondness: During that brief period he became a father—twice.

In the spring of 1949 Maria's younger sister, Carol Lane, died of tuberculosis at the age of twenty-two. Maria wrote in her biography of Nat that when she telephoned him with the news of the tragedy, his first questions were about Carol's four-and-a-half-year-old daughter, who was also named Carol but called Cookie. He wanted to adopt her. Maria, who had been extremely close to her younger sister and who, according to Kelly Cole, has difficulty talking about her to this day, agreed that they should adopt little Cookie. Everyone else in the family was in favor of the idea except for Maria's aunt Lottie. Though in her sixties, she wanted to raise Cookie herself. The Coles had to go to court to secure custody of Cookie, and naturally their relations with Dr. Charlotte Hawkins Brown were strained for years after that. Cookie was too young to understand what was happening and does not consciously remember the struggle over her.

Although Carol "Cookie" Cole does not feel that anything about her early life has been deliberately kept from her, she confesses, "I don't know when my mother died. I know when I came to live with the Coles from written sources. There are a lot of voids in my life. I was actually one of the flower girls at their wedding. My mother [Maria] won't really talk to me. . . . So, except for what I remember, I don't have a reference." Carol knows that she was born in 1944 in West Medford, Massachusetts, that her biological mother died, and that she was adopted by her aunt Maria and her uncle Nat, who became her mother and father.

Just about the time Nat and Maria completed arrangements to legally adopt Cookie, Maria discovered that she was pregnant. She had accompanied Cole and the trio on the first few dates of the Southern tour, and one of the engagements had been in Montgomery, Alabama, Nat's hometown. Maria recalled that there were "probably 276" relatives in attendance. She's certain that she became pregnant at that time. By the time the group reached North Carolina in early June, she confided to Sparky, Nat's valet, that she suspected she was pregnant. As she told the story in her book, Sparky reminded her how much Cole wanted children and suggested that she say nothing to him about it until she was sure. After Maria left the tour she went to her gynecologist, who confirmed her suspicions. Maria called Nat and told him, in a singsong voice, "You're going to be a papa." He was overjoyed.

Being an instant mother and pregnant besides didn't stop Maria from continuing to travel with her husband. She simply took Cookie along and added pregnancy to the other nuisances with which she had to cope on the road.

After the Southern tour, Cole and his trio returned to Los Angeles, where they played one- and two-week engagements at various area clubs, among them the Million Dollar Theater. The fact that they never lacked for bookings made Cole and his men unusual among small combos. By the summer of 1949 many of the "straight," or primarily instrumental, combos that had enjoyed considerable popularity in the preceding few years were having a hard time finding bookings, either because there simply were not enough "rooms" available for them or because they were asking too much money or because they played in a very specific style. According to *Billboard,* the groups that were getting work were "the all-around groups who can play for dancing from society to Latin beats." There were, however, some exceptions: "An outfit that can play bop, e.g., the George Shearing combo, can get work even tho it be limited to a handful of spots. The other exception is a King Cole who has a well established record rep."

King Cole and His Trio continued to increase that record rep in the summer of 1949. Among the releases was "I Get Sentimental Over Nothing"/"Your Voice," and a second song written by Eden Ahbez called "Land of Love." While not as commercial as "Nature Boy," it was a beautiful ballad, arranged to perfection by Pete Rugolo. On the flip side was "Yes Sir, That's My Baby," a resuscitated oldie from Cole's album released that summer, *King Cole Trio, Vol. IV*. The album itself was a combination of light jump, ballads, and a bit of bop. One of the most interesting jazz pieces was an instrumental taken from Ruggiero Leoncavallo's aria, "Ridi, Pagliaccio." Cole called it, "Laugh, Cool Clown." Jack Costanzo played in fully half the pieces but got no credit on the album cover. Capitol Records explained that the covers were stamped before it was decided which music the album would include.

Cole and his group were in an interesting transition at this time. He and his sidemen had become so popular with sweet, insinuating vocals backed by "tasteful jazz" that it was, he realized, a calculated risk to change that successful formula. Indeed, in performances at clubs where the group was practically an institution, like the Million Dollar Theater, the group stuck pretty much to their traditional style, which a writer for the *L.A. Tribune* found so polished as to be irritating. "How slick can you get!" demanded the writer. "If Nat plays bebop, he didn't include any to speak of in last week's Million Dollar program.... Where he used to be shy and diffident, Nat now purrs under applause and has grown coy.... Whatever accounts for the change—probably nothing more serious than prosperity—it's fortunate the instrumental work of the trio hasn't changed."

But Nat enjoyed bebop and the musician in him hungered for variety. Ashby's and Comfort's feelings aside, given his interest in bop he had made a wise choice in hiring Jack Costanzo, whose enthusiasm for bop was contagious even to those who didn't ordinarily take to the style. Only Costanzo shared any of the spotlight with Cole in their personal appearances. By the time King Cole and His Trio set out on their second combined tour with Woody Herman and his band in early August, they were alternating numbers like "Sweet Lorraine," "Lush Life," and "Nature Boy" with excursions into bop—"Bop Kick," "Laugh, Cool

Clown," "How High the Moon" (which had become a sort of national anthem for bebop musicians), "Cole Capers," and "Laguna Mood."

After playing twelve West Coast concerts with the Herman band, Cole and His Trio moved into Ciro's in San Francisco for a two-week booking. They played to packed houses every night, and reviewers credited Jack Costanzo's bongo playing with making them even more exciting. From there, they went to Honolulu, Hawaii.

It was their first trip to Hawaii, and they expected to do well there until they learned that the current shipping strike had seriously affected Hawaii's entertainment business—*It Happens Every Spring* at Honolulu's top first-run movie house had only 160 people in the audience at the first-night show. Worried, Carlos Gastel chose not to ask for a percentage of the gross at Honolulu's McKinley Auditorium. Instead, he asked for a flat $4000 cash in advance, plus $1,260 in plane tickets. But Gastel had misjudged the drawing power of his group and failed to recognize the difference between a first-run movie and a live concert. McKinley Auditorium was sold out most of the eight nights, and the gross was $17,562. At the usual 60 to 70 percent rate, Cole could have made between $10,500 and $12,250.

Irving Ashby remembers the trip fondly, for his salary wasn't affected by Gastel's choice of percentages. He and the two other members of the trio stayed in a little cottage across the street from the hotel where Maria and Nat roomed. "We had a jeep and a houseboy, and the buddies we met jamming over at McKinley saw to it that we had at our disposal cabin cruisers, girls, booze. We'd go 'round by Waikiki Beach, and Nat and Marie would be lying out there. We'd get in as close as we could and yell through a bullhorn, 'Hey, Nat!' And he'd look up and see us with these cruisers filled with chicks and be wishing he could be with us. Marie was cool. She'd just smile and wave."

Doris Duke, heiress to the Duke tobacco fortune, was a great fan of Cole's, and while the group was in Hawaii she asked them to play at a party at her island home. That evening she handed Cole a song a Hawaiian friend of hers had written, "Nalani." He liked it and agreed to take it to Capitol Records for recording. Released in late October, it was heavily promoted. In New York deejays were presented with leis by Judy Sinclair of the new Broadway show *Gentlemen Prefer Blondes*. Backed by "You Can't Lose a Broken Heart," the song climbed quickly on the charts.

Also in late October, *Billboard* released the results of its third annual Disk Jockey Poll, in which the King Cole Trio placed first in the Favorite Small Singing Group category. *King Cole for Kids* was voted the Favorite Children's Album. By year's end he had racked up more first-place spots in the major music polls. Lacey's, a swank Hollywood restaurant, named a room after him.

7

Uncle
Sam v.
King Cole

MARIA'S obstetrician, A. R. Arbanel, calculated February 15, 1950, as the Cole baby's due date; but Nat wasn't taking any chances on not being around for the arrival of his first natural child. During the last days of January and into the middle of February, he played engagements exclusively in L.A. He also took the opportunity to do some more recording, including two duets for Capitol with Nellie Lutcher, a collaboration arranged by Carlos Gastel, "For You My Love" was a blues song written by Paul Gayton, a bandleader; it featured Charlie Barnet on tenor sax. "It had been done by Larry Darnel on a minor label," says Lutcher, "and it was a real big record for him. At that time when a song came out on a minor label, the major labels would do a 'cover record.'" The flip side, "Can I Come in for a Minute," was a novelty song. At the time, Lutcher and her accompanist, guitarist Earl Hyde, were playing the Oasis in L.A. Cole and the trio followed her into that spot February 2 to 12 and shattered the club's attendance records.

In the midst of that engagement, Maria gave birth to their first child at Cedars of Lebanon Hospital in Los Angeles on February 6. When Maria went into labor nine days early, Nat was there at the hospital pacing nervously, as befitted a first-time expectant father. Both he and Maria had hoped for a boy, since they already had Cookie, and Maria reported that when she learned the baby was a girl, she cried. She thought her husband would be disappointed.

On the contrary, when his child was presented to him, Cole wasn't concerned about its sex. He was overcome at once with relief that the delivery had gone smoothly and with the awareness that the tiny infant was a new life he'd helped bring into the world. In 1950, at ager 32, he was old for a first-time father, but he'd dreamed of that moment for years. "I felt something impossible for me to explain in words," he told *Ebony*. "Then when they took her away, it hit me. I got scared all over again and began to feel giddy. Then it came to me—I was a father." When he visited Maria, he hastened to assure her that another daughter was fine with him. "Girls stick closer to home," he told her, "and truthfully, the moment I heard it was a girl, all the past feelings [about wanting a boy] went away. I'm happy." The sales of Nat's recording of "Yes Sir, That's My Baby" spurted around that time.

Nat and Maria had talked about boy's names often, about girl's names rarely. At first they decided to call the baby Natalie Marie. The next day they changed it to Stephanie Maria. Finally, after a third conference, they settled on Natalie Maria. *Ebony* and other sources celebrated the little girl's good fortune to be born to wealthy and talented parents.

Natalie, who was called Sweetie from the first, was barely five weeks old when Maria went back on the road with her husband. In her biography of Nat, Maria says that she discussed the matter with her doctor and that he urged her to accompany Nat on tour if she wanted to do so. He told her that the girls wouldn't need her when they were sixteen, and Maria interpreted that to mean that they wouldn't miss her when they were small. She left Cookie and Sweetie at home with a nurse and "never had a guilty conscience about it." She was so in love with Nat, she says, that she couldn't bear to be separated from him.

Natalie was just over three months old when Maria, with the help of her husband, began to plan seriously for her own comeback as a singer.

On May 11 she recorded five vocal duets with Nat for Capitol, backed by the trio, Pete Rugolo's Orchestra, and Alyce King's Vokettes. One week later, they recorded five more sides. None of them was released in the United States. One of the songs was titled "A Woman's Got a Right," and Maria certainly had a right to resume her career, baby or no baby. It's interesting, however, that she chose to resume her career so soon after Natalie's birth. One wonders if the birth of her child spurred her to attend to her own career in earnest because she suddenly felt trapped. And it's interesting, too, that Nat helped her, given his earlier strong feelings against a "two-career family." He didn't confide his reasons to anyone, as far as is known, but perhaps he was so happy about the birth of his first natural child that he was willing to do anything to please his wife.

Maria didn't actually go onstage for several months after recording the ten sides with Nat. One reason may have been that she became pregnant again. She continued to accompany Nat on the road, however, and miscarried when Natalie was nine months old.

Geri Branton feels that Maria accompanied Nat because "She had to watch her treasure. She didn't want anybody else to get him the way she had. She told Frances [Williams, the actress-activist who had been the first black to run for the California legislature in 1948] that once. Frances asked her, 'Why do you sit up here in the cold every night like this?' And Maria said, 'The way I got him?'" She was referring, no doubt, to the fact that Nat was married, and on the road without his wife, when she began dating him.

The treasure that Nat King Cole represented was not as glittering as the public might have assumed, and perhaps that's one reason Maria felt she had to travel with him and to keep abreast of his business affairs. Some time in the late winter–early spring of 1949 to 1950, the Internal Revenue Service (IRS) had contacted Cole to inform him that he owed approximately one hundred fifty thousand dollars in back taxes.

In her book, Maria suggests that their moving into Hancock Park against the wishes of their wealthy and influential white neighbors may have had something to do with the interest of the IRS in Cole's tax situation. She does not, however, imply that he was framed.

It is also possible that Cole was under particular scrutiny by the government at this time because he was a prominent black. It was the

time of the McCarthy hearings and the "Red Scare," when many prominent blacks, Jews, and other whites with possible left-leaning tendencies,
even sympathies, found themselves under the government's microscope.
Black entertainers who had championed leftist causes suffered greatly at
this time. Lena Horne was blacklisted from movies and television because
she had been associated with controversial causes. Paul Robeson, a
particular target, was denied a passport and forced to become an expatriot
for eight years. Nat King Cole had pointedly avoided controversy and
was never blacklisted. Yet, he also refused to shun people just because
they had been blacklisted. "He was always loyal to Paul Robeson," says
Geri Branton. "Unlike many people, he remained friendly and kind to
him. He went out of his way to visit Paul in a clinic in England."

Aware that Cole was maintaining friendships with people who had
been blacklisted, people who were suspected of communist leanings, the
government might have subjected him to special scrutiny. The IRS might
have decided to take a closer look at his tax returns. But again, there is no
evidence that he was framed.

Cole owed the money the government claimed he did.

"Like most entertainers," says Geri Branton, "if Nat earned ten thousand dollars, he'd spend twenty thousand dollars." There were all his staff
salaries, agents' and managers' fees, travel and housing and tips. Add to
these expenses the mortgage on their house, the decorator's fees, their
1949 Cadillac, Maria's jewelry, their clothing, Nat's noted generosity,
and his lack of concern about such things as accounting methods and
budgets, and it's not hard to imagine how he got into tax trouble. "You
can make so much money in this business that it loses all value," he once
explained to a reporter from *Ebony*. "I learned the hard way. I had my
little follies. I was, what you might say, conned out of a lot of money, and
I gave a lot of it away. But when I got in that trouble, I got the message. All
of us get the message, sooner or later. If you get it before it's too late or
before you're too old, you'll pull through all right."

Initially, Maria says, they were able to make a deal with the government under which Nat agreed to begin paying both current and back
taxes; in a year he'd paid the IRS approximately $66,000 from his
$200,000 earnings. Given all his other expenses, that didn't leave Cole

The "Prince of the Ivories" at
the Capitol recording studio, c.
1943. (Duncan Schiedt Collection)

(top) The King Cole Trio with songwriter Johnny Mercer at Capitol studios in Los Angeles. *(Duncan Schiedt Collection)*

(left) Oscar Moore, here at the Capitol studio, was an original member of the trio formed in fall 1937. Of his first meeting with Nat he said, "He looked like a real mean guy—his eyes almost closed, glintin' out at you, diggin' what was goin' on." *(Duncan Schiedt Collection)*

At Capitol's recording studio, 1943 or 1944. *(Duncan Schiedt Collection)*

(below) Cole won his first fame as a jazz pianist and retains his reputation as one of the most influential of jazz instrumentalists. *(Duncan Schiedt Collection)*

NAT COLE
SOLO
IN THE COOL OF THE DAY
IN THE COOL OF THE
DAY WHEN LOVE IS WARM WE'D BET-TER BE
WISE FOR JEAL-OUS EYES ARE ALL A- ROUND US BUT THE COOL OF THE
NIGHT IS RIGHT FOR TWO NO FOOL IN
NIGHT CAN KEEP OUR DREAM FROM COM-ING TRUE SOME-DAY
FIND THAT FAR OFF LAND WHERE LOV-ERS
KISS AND WAN-DER HAND IN HAND AND EV-RY
ONE WILL UN-DER-STAND

(facing page) An accomplished songwriter himself, as well as a pianist and singer, Nat sold his song "Straighten Up and Fly Right" in the 1930s to a music publisher on Hollywood's Vine Street for $50—outright, with no royalties. And he was grateful for the money he got. (N. Kelly Cole collection)

(below) The King Cole Trio: Nat Cole, Oscar Moore on guitar, and Wesley Price on bass. (Duncan Schiedt Collection)

Nat „King" Cole

(facing page) When Nat and his family sought to move into a monied white neighborhood, residents who wanted no blacks at all nearby complained of "flashy dress" and "zoot suits." *(Duncan Schiedt Collection)*

Maria was able to convince Nat to dress more conservatively. *(James Haskins collection)*

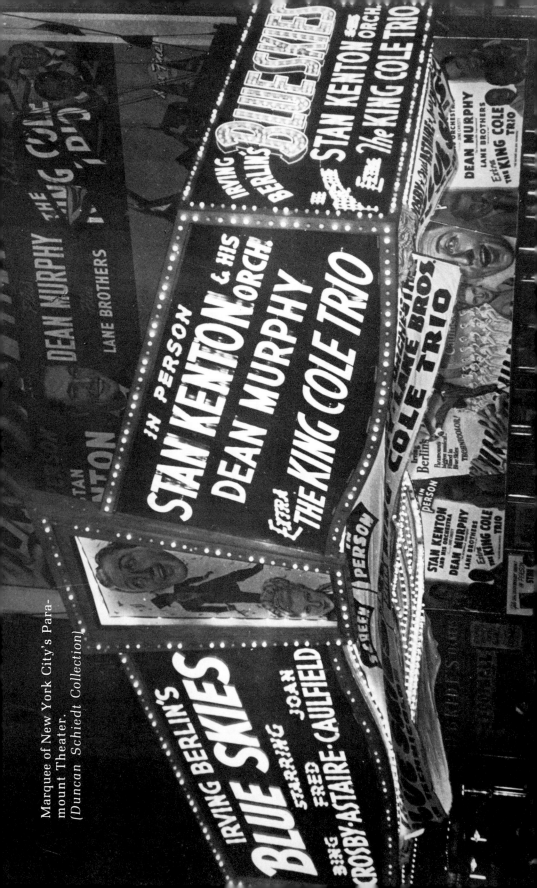

Marquee of New York City's Paramount Theater. (Duncan Schiedt Collection)

(above) The trio at the Paramount. *(Duncan Schiedt Collection)*

(below) Prior to a Carnegie Hall concert in 1949. Left to right: a Belgian critic, Woody Herman, and Nat Cole. *(Duncan Schiedt Collection)*

Nat before a Carnegie Hall concert. In just a few months the Internal Revenue Service would move against him for $150,000 in back taxes. *(Duncan Schiedt Collection)*

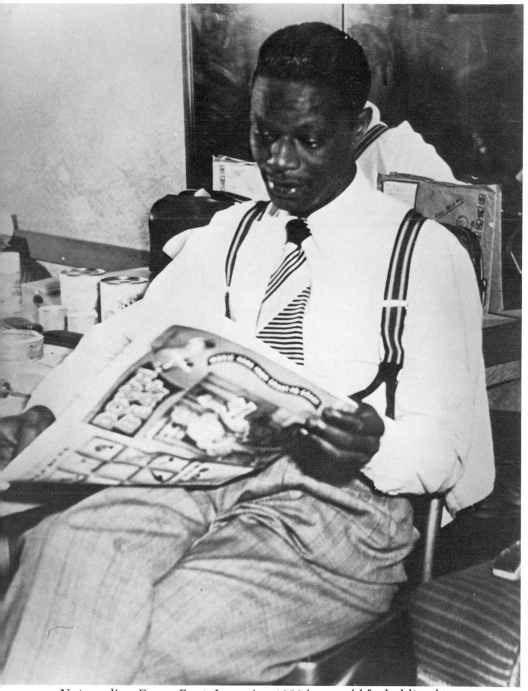

Nat reading *Down Beat*. In spring 1956 he would feel obliged to publish a letter in that magazine defending himself against charges of insufficient zeal in denouncing the sorts of bigots who had physically attacked him on stage in Birmingham, Alabama. *(Duncan Schiedt Collection)*

Realizing his long-held ambition, "The Nat 'King' Cole Show" aired for the first time in September 1956, on NBC-TV. *(N. Kelly Cole collection)*

In the face of racial hostility and sponsor fears, the time slot of the series was changed before the show finally folded in December 1957. *(James Haskins collection)*

Nat wanted to be in films even more than he'd wanted to be on television. In 1957 he was cast as a French foreign legionnaire in 20th Century-Fox's *China Gate*, playing opposite Lee Van Cleef, Gene Barry, and Angie Dickinson. The movie told the story of a small band of legionnaires trying to reach a hidden communist munitions dump. *(N. Kelly Cole collection)*

In 1959, Cole played Julie London's beleaguered uncle in a film in which a wealthy San Franciscan (John Drew Barrymore) unwittingly marries a quadroon (London) and scandalizes himself and his family when her racial heritage is revealed. *(N. Kelly Cole collection)*

Stricken with lung cancer, Nat King Cole died when he was only
45 years old, February 15, 1965. *(N. Kelly Cole collection)*

much left over. Among the obligations he "let slide" were his alimony payments to his first wife, Nadine. But interest on back taxes continued to accrue, and by the end of 1950 he owed $146,000 in current and back taxes. Early in 1951 his attorney offered the IRS $50,000 on account, but the revenuers refused the offer. It was March 1951, and Cole and Maria were in Philadelphia when they learned that the government had seized both their Cadillac and their house. They canceled a Canadian tour, caught the next flight back to Los Angeles, and faced the most humiliating experience of their lives.

The story of the seizure of their home had already hit the newspapers. An attorney on the same plane introduced himself and offered to help in any way he could. Phil Braunstein, who was based in New York, and his partner on the West Coast, Harold Plant, specialized in the business affairs of entertainers. They were able to work out an arrangement between Cole and the IRS but not before the Coles were subjected to a considerable amount of heartache. Their home was plastered with signs announcing the government seizure, newspapers gave the story wide coverage; IRS investigators made little attempt to conceal their glee at taking Nat King Cole, Negro star, down a peg or two. As if all this were not enough, that same month Nadine filed suit against her former husband, charging that he hadn't made any alimony payments to her since the end of November.

The IRS had priority over an ex-wife, and Cole's problems with the government had priority in his life for the next several weeks. Eventually Braunstein and Plant were able to work out a complicated arrangement with the IRS; and with the help of Maria's aunt and Capitol Records Cole was able to keep his part of the agreement. For the initial $50,000 payment, Maria went to her aunt. Although Aunt Lottie had gone to court against them over custody of Cookie, she had no intention of having a member of her family impoverished by the government. She gave Maria the $50,000.

It was no easy task for Maria to go to her aunt to appeal for money; and it is a testament to her love for her husband and family, as well as for the life-style to which she had become accustomed, that she made the necessary sacrifice of her pride.

Capitol Records also came through. Under a new contract, the company guaranteed Cole $120,000 in advances over a period of four years. The $30,000 guaranteed for each year of the contract would be paid directly to the government. In the event that Cole's royalty earnings exceeded $30,000 in any given year, the additional money was to be held in a deferred payment account so as not to accrue additional tax obligations to Cole. Further, Cole agreed to pay the IRS $1,000 per week out of his own pocket.

The Coles got their Cadillac back, and the IRS took the seizure signs off their house. Cole settled his problems with Nadine and resumed regular support payments to her. But it was nearly four years before he fully satisfied his tax obligations to the government. Three and a half years later, he still owed $91,000 in current and back taxes. He'd continued his string of hit records, and his deferred payment account at Capitol Records had amounted to $100,000. The IRS wanted it. Cole's accountants pointed out that if he collected that money, it would be counted as ordinary income and only increase his current tax obligations. Cole had to take out a bank loan for $90,000, use it to pay off the government, and pay back the bank with monies he withdrew periodically from his deferred payment account at Capitol.

Cole was not the first or the last entertainer, black or white, to get into tax trouble; but in later years the government seems to have been willing to settle for less. Rarely is an entertainer forced to pay his or her entire obligation these days. Cole paid every cent.

When at last they satisfied their debt to the government, neither the Coles nor the IRS agents with whom they had dealt could believe that they had actually managed to do it. The whole episode had been a nightmare, and according to Maria Cole the only time she ever saw her husband unable to sleep at night was when he was worrying about his tax problems. In such a situation, most people in Cole's position would have blamed their managers and accountants and attorneys and with good reason, since these people usually were paid to take care of such financial affairs. But Maria quotes Carlos Gastel as saying, with some amazement, "He could have blamed me, he could have blamed his accountants, but he didn't. When it happened, all he said was 'It was my own fault.'" Cole's refusal to harbor resentment was one reason he continued to be one of the best-liked people in show business, the one man who, many marveled, had no enemies.

The problems Cole had with the IRS were enough to make even the most spiritually and artistically inclined person become concerned about money, and perhaps that's one reason Nat became "more commercial" in the early 1950s. Although Jack Costanzo became a permanent member of the group, he wasn't given the opportunity to lead the trio into any new musical directions. He continued to inject what critics called freshness into the group's sound, but his job ceased to be to provide any bebop influence to speak of. Bebop was insufficiently commercial. In March 1950 Earl Wilson reported that Cole, when asked if bebop was dead, quipped, "It's not dead because it's never been alive." Instead, Costanzo provided the calypso flavor that had become the latest rage, along with its chief purveyor, Harry Belafonte.

This "commercialism," or willingness to supply what the market demanded, kept the group working steadily at the Paramount in New York, at the Thunderbird in Las Vegas, at the Fairmont and Ciro's in San Francisco. These venues attracted very different audiences, but thanks to Cole's high level of showmanship the group was as well received by bluebloods as it was by hipsters. The group's commercialism also kept Cole's record sales up: His recording of "Mona Lisa," introduced in an Alan Ladd film, *Captain Carey U.S.A.,* and winner of an Academy Award for Best Song, was a huge hit in 1950, selling more than a million copies. Maria had objected to his recording the song, feeling that an offbeat thing about an old painting wouldn't go, and Carlos Gastel had agreed; but Cole had insisted, and he proved to be right. The song was one of Nelson Riddle's earliest hit arrangements. Arrangers didn't receive label credit in those days, only bandleaders-conductors, but Riddle broke tradition and publicly claimed recognition for his work.

Cole's recording of "Too Young" was the number one song of 1951 on jukeboxes, in record sales, and in radio plays. But his commercialism caused jazz critics to cool noticeably in their assessment of the trio's success as musicians. Some critics' reviews were replete with such innuendoes as "sale-wise selection of pops, standards and a medley of the leader's vocal hits." Other reviewers, however, were more generous.

Wrote one, "The cry we've heard around is that Cole is commercial, which is always aimed at anyone who becomes successful."

Another reason (besides his problems with the IRS) why Cole may have chosen to deemphasize progressive jazz in his group's performances was their experience on their first trip to Europe in 1950. Cole had never been abroad before, and naturally he wanted to increase his following, not to mention his foreign record sales. By the late 1940s reports from across the Atlantic were hailing the popularity of jazz in Europe. In the summer of 1948 *The Valley Times,* a North Hollywood newspaper, quoted a record executive as saying of the Europeans he'd encountered during a three-month visit, "Dizzy Gillespie and Charlie Parker are their favorites in the 'Bop' class, while other big favorites of various types of jazz are Stan Kenton, King Cole Trio, Benny Goodman, Louis Armstrong, Artie Shaw and Duke Ellington." In the spring of the same year the *Everett* (Washington) *Herald* had quoted Alida Valli, a transplanted Italian actress, as saying, "The wealthy class in Rome ... have regular hot jazz sessions where they sit around and listen to Dizzy Gillespie, the King Cole Trio, Benny Goodman, and Artie Shaw." Hearing that he was popular in Europe, Cole went to see for himself.

In September 1950, accompanied by his usual entourage, including Maria, Carl Carruthers, and Mort Ruby (Sparky was not along on that trip), Cole went to London where he enthralled European jazz musicians. The general public, however, was unmoved. Apparently the Britishers were not as enamored of jazz as Cole had been led to expect. The musicians' support notwithstanding, Cole and his group did not go over well at the Palladium where they followed Lena Horne, whose two-week stint had been highly successful. Although Cole received applause for his songs that had been hits in England—songs like "Nature Boy" and "Mona Lisa"—the instrumental numbers failed to register. Derek Boulton reported in *Down Beat,* "During his act many of the elderly folk in the theater were seen leaving. This occurred mostly during Jack Costanzo's bongo solo." For much of the first week, Nat changed his program around nightly, trying to find numbers that would be appreciated by Palladium audiences. He was largely unsuccessful. Val Parnell, manager of that theater, told the British music publication *Melody Maker* that jazzmen didn't pay.

Irving Ashby remembers that London trip as the time when Nat became further separated from the men of his trio, because of his English manager. "His name was Wally something—pip-pip and all that. He was red-faced, had broken veins in his nose, tipped a whole lot at the gentlemen's club but wouldn't take a drink in front of you because he 'didn't drink.' When we first arrived, Nat wanted us all to stay at the Royal. This English manager took him aside. Carl was adjusting Maria's luggage or something, and he heard, 'Over here, we don't stay in the same hotel with our help.' Nat says, 'What help?' The guy says, 'Aren't these men working for you?'

"Maria must have been overjoyed to hear that. She'd been trying to get Nat to stop being so tight with us guys. Maria wanted to make him the Big Wheel and have us be the serfs under him. So when we got to England and the manager said we were Nat's 'help,' that backed her up. From that moment on, that's the way it was. While they stayed at the Royal, we stayed at some service apartments on St. James Place.

"We traveled in separate Rolls Royces. In one were Nat and Maria and the English manager, and there was another for us and the valet and our personal road manager and all the instruments and costumes. We had always traveled as a unit until we got over there. Returning to the United States, we took the *Queen Mary.* It was made quite clear that we were to be in cabin class and Nat and Maria would be in first class. Actually, it didn't matter to us what class we were in. We had a ball. We'd be out on the deck having a good time, and lo and behold! There was Nat up on the first-class deck leaning on the railing and looking down at us."

No doubt Cole spent a lot of time on that trip back pondering his lack of success with the English public. He returned to the United States even more persuaded that if he were to continue to be successful, he would have to become more commercial and aim his music at a larger audience. What did he mean by commercial? He once put it very succinctly— "More singing, less playing." He was also glib at times in responding to critics of his trend toward greater commercialism. "Critics don't buy records, they get 'em free." But when he was in a more thoughtful and talkative mood, he would point out that his singing style and the kinds of songs he liked to do best just happened to be enjoying more popularity than instrumentals. The gimmick songs so popular during the war years and after had palled on the public. Bebop, perhaps in part because the public never clearly understood it in the first place, was no longer as popular as it had been in 1949. Ballads, and in particular ballads sung by black crooners, had been increasingly popular since the huge success of Billy Eckstine beginning in 1945. In fact, the *Los Angeles Mirror* had reported in January 1949 that "Record companies are dickering with Herb Jeffries, Nat King Cole and others in an attempt to cash in on the craze for Eckstine. Negro vocalists, long tops in the jazz field, have seldom been top contenders in the singing of sweet ballads. Eckstine is giving the Crosbys and Comos a run for the money now." More than four years later, Cole made a remark that seemed to fulfill that prophecy: "In the last two years ballads have become favorite and quite consistently. Luckily for me, they're the songs I do best."

There was no question that Cole was a master of the ballad or that he enjoyed sentimental songs. One night at Ciro's in August 1953 he sang sixteen numbers, acceding to numerous audience requests—"It's Almost like Being in Love," "Because You're Mine," "Walking My Baby Back Home," "Somewhere Along the Way," "That's My Girl," "Pretend," "Get Your Kicks on Route 66," "Mona Lisa," "Too Young," "Calypso Blues," "Little Girl," "It's Only a Paper Moon," "Nature Boy," "Too Marvelous," "Unforgettable," "On the Sunny Side of the Street." Certainly he sang on and on to please the audience, but he may also have been pleasing himself.

Irving Ashby and Joe Comfort were not so happy about Cole's trend to greater commercialism. Says Ashby, "Nat's voice wasn't all that great— he hit the right note at the right time—but he was a doggone good musician." Comfort also felt that Cole was hurting himself by playing less music: "He could play anything, drive the average piano player crazy. I loved him. Before I joined him, I knew just about every song he played, had all his records. I just loved his sound, and it made me mad when he stopped playing and started singing. He was a musician's musician."

Still, the two remained with him. They liked Nat King Cole. "He was a real nice guy to work for," says Comfort. "I only saw him get mad— really mad—one time. Somebody got loaded and wasn't playing right, made some mistakes. When we got back to the dressing room, Nat just laid it out. But he waited until we were in the dressing room, he didn't do it onstage."

There's no question that Maria encouraged Nat's increasing commercialism. If Cole did not actually give credit to Maria for the musical style of his group, he gave her credit for much else. Asked by *Ebony,* "Are second marriages better?" he called her "the chancellor of my exchequer who has balanced my budget," credited her with giving him more confidence to become aggressive in demanding better terms from theater and club managers and, in general, for "transforming his life": "Commercially, musically, and psychologically I am a much-improved man. I have a greater urge for wholesome hobbies like golf and photography and spend more time at them. I hate to appear immodest, but marrying Maria was a major stroke of genius. I have gained more than I can say."

Some members of Cole's trio didn't share his enthusiasm about Maria's ability to balance his budget, for they believed she was doing it at their expense. Comfort recalls, "She said to Nat right in front of us, 'You're paying them too much. Stan Kenton's men don't get that much money. You're the star...' and so on. She even got rid of our road manager, Mort Ruby, because she said he was handling too much money. She wanted to do the managing, handle the money."

Says Ashby, "It was very hush-hush about who made what. There wasn't the same closeness as when he was with Oscar Moore and Johnny Miller. It was a three-way split with them—thirty-thirty-forty. When the personnel started changing, that stopped. When I took over Oscar's job, he was getting nine hundred dollars base pay a week. I got three hundred and fifty dollars a week. There was extra money for extra work— recording or appearing on Johnny Carson's or Ed Sullivan's shows. We paid our own hotel bills, but they paid all travel expenses. In those days, that was pretty good money." But it was not so great that they felt Maria had any reason to begrudge it to them.

The crisis came when Cole, because of his tax problems, decided it was necessary to cut his sidemen's pay. "We would be getting less than half," says Comfort. "I told him that instead of cutting our salaries, he should raise them and that would cut down on the taxes he owed. He said he didn't know if he could do that."

They were appearing at Lake Tahoe at the time. Ashby recalls, "I'm watching him gamble at the roulette tables—ten thousand dollars, fifteen thousand dollars at a throw—just having fun. But if he had that kind of money to throw away, he had a hell of a nerve to come out of the casino and call a meeting of the guys in the group and confront us with the fact that he's going to have to cut our salaries because of his taxes.

"Another thing that kind of soured us: Stan Kenton was also in a tax bind. He took his whole orchestra to South America and told them that when they got back to the United States they were each to pick out a new car. He would make the down payment for them. Carlos Gastel was always booking us together, and that whole band had new cars. Kenton solved his tax problem—wrote off all those down payments. Nat, instead of giving us something, was trying to take it away."

Ashby submitted his two weeks' notice immediately. "I told him in my notice that I was leaving because the job wasn't a challenge anymore. I had students who could do the job. What I really wanted to say was that I wasn't doing anything for me. Here I was watching a guy who could throw away fifteen thousand dollars in one spin of a roulette wheel and wishing he'd just give me that much for a bonus at Christmastime."

Ashby started free-lancing and worked with Oscar Peterson, among others. He also worked with Ernie Freeman, an arranger, copying music. He is now retired. John Collins traveled out from New York to take over Ashby's job with the trio. "Nat had wanted Wes Montgomery, but he couldn't get him," says Carl Carruthers. "He got John from Art Tatum."

Joe Comfort left the trio around the same time as Ashby did. "I went with Nelson Riddle," he says. "Nobody had really heard of Nelson Riddle before Nat. He arranged a lot of those string tunes. With Nelson, I recorded with Sinatra on his second comeback, Peggy Lee, Ella Fitzgerald, Sy Oliver. . . . I also made some recordings with Nat after I left, for the album *Love.*" Comfort's job was taken over by Charles Harris, who had played with Lionel Hampton. Before Comfort left, Cole took Harris along to La Vie en Rose in New York to give him experience with the group. Jack Costanzo remained with the trio.

By now the trio was a mere shadow of its former self, and so many changes in personnel did little to maintain Cole's loyalty to his sidemen. Rumors began to circulate that Cole would disband the trio altogether, and in late August 1951 Carlos Gastel confirmed those rumors. Effective immediately, Gastel announced, the trio would not be featured with Cole, and Cole would receive sole billing. Cole's three musicians were free to leave, and in future engagements he would be able to work with any threesome he wanted. He would do little or no recording with any trio in the future, preferring the successful formula of production numbers arranged by Les Baxter and Peter Rugolo.

Gastel's announcement proved to be both premature and misleading, however. Cole found that he preferred the familiar trio arrangement and liked to work with the same group of musicians. In late February 1952, critic Leonard Feather happily announced in *Down Beat,* "King Cole Trio Isn't Dead." Feather's review of the group at L.A.'s Tiffany club was laudatory except when he wrote about Jack Costanzo. "We'd prefer to forget that Jack Costanzo was there," he wrote. "On many items he seemed entirely superfluous and enough aware of it to keep pretty much in the background."

Jack Costanzo left the group that year. He was replaced briefly by Charlie Blackwell, younger brother of Bumps Blackwell. Charlie Blackwell had played two years with Benny Carter and then with Stan Kenton and with both groups had often appeared on the same bill as Cole and the trio. He learned bongo drum playing from Costanzo. "Jack decided to go out on his own, form his own band," says Blackwell, "so when he got ready to leave Nat he brought Nat to the club in San Diego where I was playing with Walter Fuller's band and said that I should replace him. I worked with Nat for a short while—seven or eight weeks in L.A.—but then I decided I wanted to sing. When you were with Nat King Cole, you *didn't* sing. I wanted to do my own thing, so I got myself a little group." Drummer Bunny Shawker joined the group briefly, but eventually Lee Young, brother of tenor sax man Lester Young, became the trio's drummer. He had played in the early Jazz at the Philharmonic concerts. The new trio—John Collins on guitar, Charles Harris on bass, and Lee Young on drums—did background for Nat's vocals and usually merged into big bands when he played major dates or recorded.

During the summer and fall of 1952, Cole cut down on his performing schedule, announcing that he was on a semi vacation. His daughters were beside themselves with joy. While Nat and Maria were on the road, Cookie and Sweetie stayed in Hancock Park and were cared for by a nurse. Carol, who attended the nearby Thirty-second Street elementary school and actually integrated it, being the first black to enroll there, remembers that their first nurse, whom they called Nana, was named Vera Mae Flowers. Maria's sister, Charlotte Sullivan, whom the girls called Barba, was "really in charge of everything," says Carol. "She oversaw everything when they were on the road, and they were on the road a great deal. She didn't live with us, but she was Dad's private secretary for eight years, and being the sister and all, she was there every day. She was the one, if no one else could be contacted, who would have the authority to give the final say. She was the one who showed up at PTA meetings and attended various school events when our parents were not available."

Carol recalls, "It's not easy to have parents who are on the road. How could we keep them close? I think the reason why I love to write letters is that it was the most I could do to communicate with them. When they would come home, Natalie and I would put on little shows for them. We'd make them sit down, and I would do a dance, and Sweetie would sing and sometimes we would lip-sync." She remembers his laughter: "It was unique. If you knew him, the minute you heard it you knew who it was. The sound didn't come from his belly so much as his throat, a scratching kind of sound. And he had a gesture—cocking his chin and kind of scratching his hand back toward the chin—that was totally his."

The times when Cole eased up on his performing schedule, as he did during the summer and fall of 1952, are special times in Carol's memory. No doubt they were special for Cole as well. For a man who had wanted children as badly as he, it was difficult to be away from the home and family life he'd worked so hard to have.

8

Looking
for a
Way Out

OLE was back on his usual ambitious schedule by early 1953, when he was involved in breaking a temporary eighteen-month agreement among Las Vegas hotel operators not to raid each other for talent. Cole and the trio played El Rancho for $4,500 a week and were so successful that his manager asked for a higher salary for a return date. When the owners of El Rancho declined, Gastel went to Jack Entratter at the Sands. Entratter signed Cole at $12,500 a week for a three-week stretch each year for three years beginning in January 1954.

Cole's part in the matter showed an increased aggressiveness in business. But aggressiveness was not Nat's natural style, and along with his problems with the IRS, his attempts to be more forthright in his demands for money and better working conditions may have contributed to his habit of biting his fingernails to the quick and smoking three or four packs of unfiltered cigarettes a day until, according to Irving Ashby, they

123

burned his fingers. Geri Branton remembers that Cole was never without a cigarette. Both the anxiety and the nicotine ate away at his stomach, and he began to feel pain. When Joe Comfort was a member of the trio, he doesn't remember Nat's having problems with his stomach, but, he says, "I wasn't surprised when I heard, because the tension that man went through was awful—the nagging!"

On Easter Sunday, April 5, 1953, Cole and his trio, Billy May and his orchestra, and Sarah Vaughan were scheduled to perform two shows at Carnegie Hall to kick off a long joint concert tour. But Cole's brief appearance onstage during the second show was not to sing. It was to announce that he could not perform because he had to go to the hospital. Backstage between shows he had been struck by an attack of bleeding ulcers. At New York Hospital doctors removed half of Cole's stomach. He spent five weeks there. While recuperating at home in Los Angeles, he came down with food poisoning and lost seventeen pounds. He was on a soft-food diet for four months. During that time, on doctor's orders, he quit smoking, but as soon as his stomach, or what was left of it, had fully healed, he went back to his old habit, making the concession of using a three-inch cigarette holder.

Carol Cole remembers the period of her father's recuperation as another one of the happy times of her childhood. Natalie was only about three-and-a-half, and so when he went out, she didn't accompany her father as often as Carol did. She remembers days when "Dad and I would go to record stores in South L.A. and pick up Moms Mabley and Redd Foxx albums. I've often thought that my father would have adored Richard Pryor and Eddie Murphy. He really supported those kinds of people, and I think it may have been because of his background—his childhood in Chicago. Because of his life and celebrity, he wasn't able to stay as close to that element as he would have liked.

"Being with him at those times is one of my favorite memories. I felt as if I'd come into the world to be there for those moments."

It was a time of introspection for Cole, a time when he reviewed his life. Losing half of his stomach gave him intimations of mortality and caused him to think about his priorities. Cole had come from humble beginnings and achieved fame and fortune beyond his wildest expectations; but in the process he'd lost touch with his roots, not to mention his health. He seems to have concluded that the struggle hadn't been worth the cost. Friends and acquaintances recall that the illness left him morose and that he was quieter and more moody from that time on.

He was at the height of his success, and he could have quit the business or drastically curtailed his performing schedule. But he had enormous responsibilities—the house in Hancock Park, a wife who enjoyed luxury, two small children, as well as a still-large debt to the government. His determination to meet his responsibilities left him few options but to continue working hard, with all the tensions that work entailed.

Cole's illness may have had something to do with his blossoming interest in doing films. Film work was far less grueling than work as a touring musical entertainer. That year he sang the theme song for *Hajji Baba,* Walter Wanger's film starring John Derek and Elaine Stewart. Wanger and Cole liked each other immediately, and Wanger, who was a longtime fan of Cole's music, suggested that they work together on other films. As reported by Hollywood columnists, Wanger wanted Cole to costar either with Humphrey Bogart or James Cagney in a Richard English espionage thriller. Cole would play a singer and piano player in a café (à la Dooley Wilson in *Casablanca*). But Cole's would be a fuller character—his singer–piano player would also be a government agent. For Cole, whose previous film parts had not been integral to the story line, this was a great chance—for once his singing would be pertinent to the plot.

Around that same time he was contacted about playing the title role in a remake of the film version of Eugene O'Neill's *Emperor Jones,* and this was even more to his liking. O'Neill's emperor was a solid dramatic role, the singing incidental to the story. Coproducer Burgess Meredith was reportedly very much in favor of Cole for the part, but in the end the project was dropped. Walter Wanger's plans bore no fruit either. The fall of 1953 saw Cole on the road as usual, heading a package deal with Sarah Vaughan for Sid Caesar's Big Show, his dreams of Hollywood film stardom shelved for the time being.

As 1954 began, Cole played the first three-week engagement for which he had contracted with the Sands Hotel in Las Vegas. Maria, Carol, and Natalie went along. The Cole children never liked Las Vegas, for a variety of reasons. One was that they felt alienated there. Carol Cole remembers "hating Las Vegas and being very fearful, very frightened. Those early days at the Sands I remember being in such a totally white environment. In those days it was really odd to see any blacks in the casinos. We [blacks] were only visible cleaning up in the kitchen." But Maria insisted on accompanying her husband there and on taking the children whenever possible. She may have regarded them as allies in her determination to keep Cole groupies at bay in that most licentious atmosphere. There were a lot of temptations in Las Vegas.

Few black entertainers played the Sands, and Cole's appearance there could have been a PR man's dream; but his shows were not widely covered. Kelly Cole feels that this was his mother's doing. "She's a classy lady, and she would have wanted things to be very discreet. She would have gone to the press people and said, 'I don't want this played up. We're there and we're just going to pretend we're like everyone else.'" The engagement was uneventful except for the time when Carol and Natalie decided to go to the hotel dining room for breakfast and were barred from the room. "Mom was not so discreet then," says Kelly. "She has *a temper!*" But she dealt with the problem directly and didn't take her grievances to the press.

A major topic of discussion in the world of entertainment that year was the impact of television on live entertainment, particularly in clubs and theaters. In a comical piece written from New York and carried by *Melody Maker,* a British music publication, A. William Lovelock elaborated on the threat posed by the "evil eye" of American show business:

"Nat Cole flew into a strangely subdued city when he arrived here from Hollywood a few weeks back. The bubble of night life had burst. Well-known night spots were closing down, old-established bars were on the real estate market, and not *one* movie theatre throughout the length of Broadway was employing a house orchestra. . . . And in two million rooms scattered across the island from Brooklyn Bridge to Harlem, the missing club clientele sat in the darkness, hushed and tongue-tied, hypnotised by the evil eye that put the hex on New York's famous night life . . . television!"

Nat Cole was working—he and his trio were booked into La Vie en Rose on East Fifty-fourth Street. But there were a lot of groups and individual musicians who were not so fortunate. Television was indeed changing the shape of entertainment in the United States. Cole could see the trend. While films were the medium to which he was attracted most, he also liked the idea of doing television. He appeared on Ed Sullivan's *Toast of the Town* while in New York and had his agents working on the possibility of his having a regular series of his own, similar to the Wildroot-sponsored radio show that had run sixty-eight weeks some years back. But regular work on television was even less definite than film work for Cole. For the time being he had only his recording and concert work, and perhaps to keep from being bored, he decided to try Europe again.

The trip was months in the planning, primarily because when he first applied for permission to perform in Britain he was informed that he could not bring the trio. The British Musicians' Union had persuaded the Ministry of Labor not to issue work permits to American musicians, contending that allowing American musicians to perform in that country deprived British musicians of work. Their union wanted a reciprocal arrangement whereby an approximately equal number of British musicians would work in the United States, but the American Federation of Musicians wouldn't agree to that proposal; their leaders favored an "entirely free exchange of labor." In those years, when the direction of musical influences was primarily West to East, Americans were the clear beneficiaries of unrestricted access to audiences. Among British groups, only Ted Heath and his orchestra enjoyed substantial popularity in the United States.

Cole was not about to perform in Europe accompanied by house bands. Somehow his people managed to get work permits issued to John Collins, Lee Young, and Charles Harris. But the process took months.

The group arrived in London on March 20, accompanied by two valets and Maria. Asked why she hadn't brought the children along, Maria said that when they had been in London before, there had been milk shortages, and she didn't know whether or not the situation had improved. Asked what she planned to do in London, she replied, "I'm doing a bit of detective work trying to track down some silver and china and a chandelier that will be suitable for our home in Los Angeles." Otherwise, she planned to do in England what she usually did while on the road with Nat—play poker with him in his dressing room between shows, appear as the King's Queen on opening nights and at social functions, and generally keep an eye on things. The Coles stayed at the Savoy Hotel, an event sufficiently noteworthy to merit an item in the *Sunday Pictorial:* "Nat 'King' Cole is coloured—and if for him to stay at the Savoy isn't a sudden ray of enlightenment in hotel management, I'll eat Nat's music, including encores." Four years earlier, Lena Horne had observed discrimination at the Piccadilly Hotel—not against herself but against some West Indian friends—and British racism had not softened appreciably since then. Indeed, a few months earlier the Savoy had operated under an unofficial ban against Negroes. Cole was that popular in England.

Since he had been there last, jukeboxes and disc jockeys had taken the country by storm, and Cole's records were regularly on the British Broadcasting Corporation (BBC) radio shows. Teenagers in line for tickets mentioned specific songs, like "Tenderly" and "Pretend," as favorites. Said one girl to a reporter from the *Wolverhampton Express and Star* who wanted to know why she was standing in line for tickets for a concert that was nearly a month away, "I've been waiting outside since half-past seven, but it will be well worth it if he sings 'Pretend.'"

Hundreds of other teenagers queued up to buy advance tickets for Cole's various scheduled concerts around Britain. Tickets for all evening shows at the London Palladium were sold out and there were few left for the afternoon matinees before Cole and his trio even arrived. Also before he arrived, the British Musicians' Union made one last attempt to enforce its policy against American musicians' taking jobs that would otherwise go to Britishers. The Musicians' Union barred the resident British orchestra at the Palladium, the Skyrockets, from playing on a stage with three American musicians.

Val Parnell, manager of the Palladium, was quick to respond to the threat; he announced that he would seek an injunction restraining the union from obstructing the Skyrockets' performance. He also threatened to sue the union for £25,000, the loss the theater would incur by refunding ticket money for Cole's two weeks of performances. Musicians' Union officials called a special meeting on Saturday, March 20, the day Cole arrived in London, to discuss the situation and decided not to press their original demand. They informed the Skyrockets that although they hadn't changed their conviction about U.S. musicians performing in Britain, they had decided to allow the orchestra to play with the Cole group after all.

For Johnny Dankworth, leader of the Skyrockets, the union's decision came as a great relief. Not only had he and his group faced being out of work for the two weeks that the Palladium would be closed; they also faced cancellation of additional bookings with Cole. "The union's policy is stupid," said Dankworth. Pointing out that Cole's visit had provided his band with extra dates, he said, "If other American musicians were allowed to play here, they would also provide work." One critic couldn't see what all the furor had been about: "At the risk of sticking our neck well and truly out in a quarrel that is none of our affair we would remark, nevertheless, that we cannot see that the absence of these gentlemen [the trio] would in this instance make much difference in Mr. Cole's act."

Cole at the Palladium (also on the bill was a British-born American comedian named Henny Youngman) was a smash success. Critics remarked often about his relaxed, polished, dignified style. Wrote Ray Sonin of *The New Musical Express,* "Nat believes in getting right down to his work. He walks smilingly on stage—a tall, rangy figure in an immaculate light-grey suit—and goes right into 'Almost like Being in Love' without any introduction. He grins in grateful acknowledgment of the yells and screams that greet his number, and straight away continues with 'Somewhere Along the Way,' followed by 'That's My Girl.' There is a white piano in front of the orchestra, and he stabs a few chords while standing up, then turns aside to sing into the stand-mike. In his next number—the unforgettable 'Unforgettable'—he plays half a chorus at the piano, but goes straight back to singing again." Wrote Tony Brown in *Melody Maker,* "He has turned what might have been an abrupt stage transition from pianist to vocalist into a prime piece of stagecraft, moving away from the piano casually, yet reaching back carelessly to one-finger an odd note or two in completion of a phrase. It is only in the last number, 'Too Marvellous for Words,' that the trio gets a real chance to register alone."

While the real music critics could detect the more advanced harmonic conception in the arrangements that distinguished Cole and his trio from

129

ordinary commercial groups, the jazz they played was too subtle to offend the "conservative elements" who had complained of a "surfeit of jazz" four years earlier. Of course, there were people who were disappointed that Cole played so little piano. One reader asked why in a question submitted to *The New Musical Express*. Cole responded, "I'd like to play more piano, too! But the general public disagrees with us. If I'm playing a concert date to an audience comprising at least fifty percent jazz fans, I still include quite a few instrumental selections. But not in theater. There, the customers want to hear my record hits—and my record hits have all been vocal."

A major complaint on this tour was that the teenagers in the galleries drowned out the first few bars of each number with their screams. Cole was rather embarrassed by this type of demonstration, which in the United States was generally reserved for white singers like Sinatra or the masters of vocal acrobatics like Johnny Ray and Frankie Laine. The crowds back home were not usually so demonstrative. As he explained to another questioner, "I've tried to think what it is. I suppose it is just mob psychology. It started with Frank Sinatra—just a gag, I believe—and it has grown into a cult."

Audience reaction was the same wherever he went in Britain and Ireland—in Newcastle upon Tyne, Dublin, Belfast, Hanley. In Glasgow, an extra matinee was arranged to accommodate all the fans. Hordes of "screaming young ladies" tried to mob him after each performance, and in Wolverton they did succeed in breaking down part of the stage door. Reinforcing bars were quickly nailed up and pushed out again by the crowd. Audience enthusiasm continued undiminished despite the fact that in performances outside the major cities, Cole injected more instrumentals into his act. But just a few. In truth Nat didn't feel he could play much piano; he was out of practice!

Cole's instrument was now his voice and so to a great extent was the microphone. One critic who previously had fought against the use of microphones in music halls wrote that he had been converted when he witnessed Cole's performance at the London Palladium: "Much the most striking aspect of his presentation is in his use of the microphone. At his call it assumes the status of a musical instrument with a virtue of its own upon which he plays with the sensitivity of a skilled, intuitive musician.

As he sings a tide of warm, dark velvet slowly floods from the loudspeakers to fill the theatre with an all-enveloping warmth of faintly exotic melody that is marked by an intriguing hint of dissonance on the falling notes." But it was the voice that turned the microphone from a tool to an instrument in its own right—the husky, dusky voice that was unforgettable. Cole defied all the singer's rules in taking care of it, or failing to do so. He chain-smoked regular Philip Morrises, although he did, now, use a cigarette holder. When he wasn't smoking a cigarette, he was smoking a pipe. He collected pipes and in Britain was presented with several to augment his collection. He never refused to grant an interview because his voice was overworked. On the contrary, he deliberately abused his voice. "I can't sing until my voice is good and hoarse," he told one interviewer. "It's the huskiness that does it. That's why I like to talk a lot. It helps me sing better."

Besides performing in eight countries and giving scores of interviews, Cole took time to enjoy a kind of "second honeymoon" with Maria. They celebrated their sixth anniversary in London and spent six days in Paris after the tour was over, sightseeing. Lena Horne and her husband Lennie Hayton were also in Paris at the time, and the two couples went sightseeing together. After nearly two months in Europe, the Coles returned to the United States on the French liner *Liberté*. The fifteen-thousand-mile tour grossed an estimated one hundred and twenty-five thousand dollars, giving Nat and Maria good cause for celebration.

While in Europe, Maria had been asked by a reporter for the *London Daily Express* if she minded having given up her career for marriage. "I never regretted it," she answered. "I guess every girl likes to see her name in lights, but I was lucky in being able to get that over when I was younger. If I were still twenty-one, I might miss it. Not now—and anyway my husband and children make a much better career." She failed to mention that before leaving for Europe she had recorded her own album, titled *A Girl They Call Maria.* Issued by Kapp Records, it constituted another effort to resume her own singing career. She was now in her early thirties; if she didn't make her comeback soon she might lose the chance altogether. There were conflicting reports, however, about whose idea it was for her to record the album. She told interviewers, "It was really his [Cole's] idea that I go back into show business." But Cole said, "My wife wants to sing so much she was even caught sing-walking in her sleep. . . . Building a home and a family took Maria away from show business. But it's no wonder, now that she's done such a good job at that, she'd like to continue with doing a good job of singing. There has been much persuasion on all sides, and finally she was convinced by Dave Kapp of Kapp Records to record again."

After returning to the United States from Europe, Maria set to work rehearsing a night club act, and on October 5, 1955, she opened at Ciro's on the Sunset Strip in Hollywood. Nat was completely supportive. The night Maria opened, he sent her two telegrams:

> If they love your act half as much as I love you then smash will be your triumph.
>
> Your Husband

> Mommy, we know you will be a big smash tonight love and kisses.
> Cookie and Sweetie

She also received a note from Gladys (Mrs. Lionel) Hampton, expressing her regret at not being able to be there. Gladys Hampton was among the few friends of the Coles' who didn't attend. It was, said Louella Parsons, a "star-studded first night." Dorothy Dandridge, Jimmy Van Heusen, Helen Grayco and Spike Jones, Pearl Bailey, Billy Daniels, Leo Durocher and Laraine Day, Richard Egan, and many others showed up to cheer Maria on. Jimmy Van Heusen gave a party in Maria's honor after the show where Dinah Washington, unable to see Maria perform because she was doing her own show at the Mocambo, sang some of her latest recordings.

Maria's thirty-minute act consisted of a variety of old and new songs and ranged from blues to sentimental numbers, most of them from her new album, *A Girl They Call Maria.* She did a comedy sketch about the Giants, the Dodgers, and Willie Mays and a humorous song, "The Wrong Mink." She sang a medley of songs made popular by Ethel Waters and several ballads of the kind for which her husband was famous, the most telling title among them being "I Want to Do What You Do."

Irv Kupcinet of the *Chicago Sun-Times* and local reporters were kind to Maria. According to Kup's column, she "scored a terrific triumph." "Last night's crowd liked her tremendously," reported the *Hollywood Citizen-News.* And Hal Landers of the *Hollywood Reporter* predicted, ". . . she may rise to rank with some of the top vocalists in her field in a short time." But the critic for *Variety* was not so generous: "Mrs. Cole . . . has aimed too high in this return to showbiz. . . . She was, and still is, a band singer—and even allowing for opening nervousness, is a long way from the stature needed to headline one of the top spots in the country."

On October 23, 1955, Maria appeared with Nat on Ed Sullivan's *Toast of the Town,* but her comeback didn't get off the ground. That same week, Nat opened at the Copacabana in New York. "Nat Cole Has Gals Squealing at Copa" read the headline of the *New York World Telegram and Sun.* He was a hard act to follow.

While her husband was alive, Maria Cole never again tried to make a comeback on the stage. She could see even unpleasant events in a positive light, and by the early 1960s she would say that her life was much too full to consider a career of her own. "It has been my observation," she told a reporter around 1963, "that the majority of women performers who go back into show business after marriage do so because there is something missing in the marriage and they do not experience the rich fulfillment of home, children and the civic demands [that] so enrich my life." If she was even aware that Maria had tried to return to the stage eight years earlier, the reporter didn't bring it up.

In honor of Nat's tenth anniversary with Capitol Records, the eleven-year-old company issued a sixteen-song anniversary LP consisting primarily of previously unrecorded songs. Side one featured Cole and the Trio, and though the personnel had changed, the sound didn't suffer. Working as usual without benefit of written arrangements, they played over the phrases a few times, then, each at his own mike, played the song, leaving the engineer to worry about balance. Some songs they did three, four, or five times, but for "Little Girl" they did just one. Side two featured Cole backed by full orchestra, and Steve Race of *Melody Maker* commented on an improvement in Cole's voice, particularly in his sostenuto [ability to sustain a note] on this side. But Race also noticed a decline in Cole's diction: "One can't help wishing his wife had kept plugging away

133

on the subject," wrote Race. "Though I grant that some of his stranger enunciations can be quite fetching, they can also be a distraction."

That year, Cole also starred as himself in a twenty-minute film titled *The Nat King Cole Story*. Released by Universal-International, it was the third in a series of short film biographies of black stars. Joe Louis's and Jackie Robinson's stories had preceded Cole's. The film was shot in two days and released to movie houses that summer. Narrated by Jeff Chandler, it covered the major events of Cole's career, including the legendary beginning of his career as a singer, the discrimination he faced as a singer of ballads when the recording of such songs by a black singer was considered inappropriate, and his attack of ulcers at Carnegie Hall. Cole sang five songs in the film, beginning with "Straighten Up and Fly Right" and ending with *"Je Vous Aime."* It was his biggest movie role to date. His popularity as a recording artist was never greater. His singles regularly appeared in the top ten; in June 1955 he became the only recording star with six record sides on the best-selling charts at one time. He also regularly broke attendance records at places like the Fairmont Hotel in San Francisco, Chez Paree in Chicago, the Copacabana in New York, and the Grove Theater in Los Angeles. Adeline Hanson did publicity for the Grove from 1955 to about 1965. "His were always sellout engagements," she says, "and he was extremely admired and liked by everybody." He was mobbed in Jamaica and Trinidad in March 1955. He was Nat King Cole and he was the king. Gradually but steadily the trio part of his act had receded into the background, along with his piano playing. "He began diminishing his piano—almost nightly," says Hanson. By the spring of 1955 he had to agree with Maria that he no longer needed a trio. For quite some time they had been little more than window dressing anyway. Hardly any of the fans who bought his records remembered that once the King Cole Trio had been famous for their jazz instrumentals. Only real jazz buffs would keep that memory alive. For most people Nat Cole was a singer who took occasional swipes at the piano keys. That spring Cole disbanded the trio, and an eighteen-year-old institution came to an end, although occasionally he revived it for tours abroad, and in 1956 he brought them in on an album that was recorded in four sessions with a variety of instrumentalists.

Called *After Midnight*, all the tracks on the album featured a fourth instrumentalist in addition to Cole on piano, Collins on guitar, Harris on bass, and Young on drums. The three tracks recorded on August 15, 1956, featured Harry Edison on trumpet. He was replaced by Willie Smith on alto sax for the three tracks recorded on September 15. Smith was replaced by Juan Tizol on trombone for the three tracks recorded on September 21; and he in turn was replaced by Stuff Smith on violin for the last three tracks, which were recorded on September 24.

In reviewing Cole's shows as a single performer, critics gave only passing attention to the fact that he had left the trio behind. And they gave his piano playing no more attention than he gave to his piano, which continued to share the spotlight with him, orphaned though it was. He now traveled with a full orchestra, one of whose members was Johnny Miller, who had been with the King Cole Trio in the mid-1940s. No other former members of the trio were in the orchestra.

It was a time of endings for Nat. Not only did he give up the group he'd had for nearly two decades, but he lost his mother that spring. She was old, and Nat had had years to make peace with the prospect of her passing, but that didn't prevent him from breaking down at the funeral. Maria was not with him. She'd not been close to her husband's family, except Eddie, from the beginning. "There was very little contact," says Kelly Cole. "We exchanged Christmas presents, but that was about it. We saw them maybe once a year. There were looked down on. Nobody said anything, but it was understood that we kept them at a distance." In a taped interview, a member of the trio says that Maria once called Nat's mother a baboon in front of Nat and his sidemen. They held the impression that the Coles were, in Maria's eyes, too dark-skinned and too low-life, and no doubt Nat suffered from conflicting feelings of guilt and shame about that for years. When his mother died, he regretted not having insisted on including her in his new life. He was melancholy for months after her death. "My greatest disappointments are too numerous to mention," he told an interviewer that spring.

9

Cole's "Race Problem"

IN February 1956, Cole toured in Australia for a week; and since Australia was a very segregated country it was useful practice for him, a way to prepare for his second tour in the South. That tour, which began in April, also featured British orchestra leader Ted Heath and his group, whose singer was June Christie; the Four Freshmen; and comedian Gary Morton. Two years earlier the U.S. Supreme Court, in the landmark *Brown vs. Topeka Board of Education* case, had outlawed segregated schools; but the racial situation in the South remained largely unchanged. In some cities, special arrangements had to be made for blacks and whites touring together and for the seating of the audiences. The tour began in the Southwest, where in San Antonio the audience was totally integrated. In Fort Worth and Houston blacks and whites sat in separate sections. In Alabama the restrictions were more rigid; blacks and whites were not allowed to appear onstage together. So, according to Carl Carruthers, who accompanied Nat on the tour, the show's road manager,

Bob Schwartz, arranged for a curtain on the stage to separate Cole and his band from Heath and his orchestra. Audiences were completely segregated as well: The first show was for whites, the second for blacks.

All went well in Mobile, but Carl Carruthers recalls that he was still nervous about Birmingham. "I told Nat something was going to happen," he says. "I tried to get him to cancel." But plans for two concerts in Birmingham on April 10 went ahead.

Three days before the concerts, the local White Citizens Council had launched a campaign against "Negro music," bebop, and rock 'n' roll as "immoral"; they charged that it was inspired by the National Association for the Advancement of Colored People as a form of "integration brainwash" for Southern white teenagers. While the only target category into which Cole fit was "Negro," a group of local men apparently decided that was sufficient. At a filling station in Anniston, Alabama, the owner and five others planned to round up some one hundred fifty friends from Anniston, Piedmont, Bessemer, Tuscaloosa, and the Birmingham area to infiltrate the audience at Cole's first concert (for whites) and to abduct Cole. But on the night of the concert, the expected mob failed to show, and only the original six actually arrived. In their car, where two of the men remained, they carried two .22-caliber pump rifles, a homemade blackjack, and brass knuckles.

Onstage, Cole had been introduced as the starring act and was launching into his third song, "Little Girl," when suddenly four men rushed the stage. A woman screamed, but Cole, blinded by the bright lights, could see nothing. Then a microphone hit him in the face, and he fell backward over his piano bench. Terrified, he allowed Carruthers to hustle him off the stage and to his dressing room. In the melee, a Birmingham policeman had his nose broken by a soda bottle, and one of the attackers, who had leaped at Cole, was beaten with a nightstick. All four attackers and the two men waiting in the car outside were arrested; the car, with its small arsenal, was impounded.

Nat's lip was bruised and his back hurt, but what pained him most was the realization that utter strangers hated him so much that they would violate the concert stage to get to him. When things calmed down out front, he returned to the stage. The audience gave him a standing ovation. "I just came here to entertain you," he said. "That was what I thought you wanted. I was born here. Those folks hurt my back. I cannot continue, because I have to go to a doctor." After an examination showed nothing broken, Cole returned to the auditorium to perform in the second concert, for blacks. But he canceled the concerts scheduled for the coming week and went to Chicago for a rest.

In those days whites who committed crimes against blacks in the South were rarely punished, but in the case of the men who had plotted against Nat Cole justice was swift—and "just." Within less than two weeks after the incident, four were convicted of conspiracy to commit assault and given maximum sentences—four months in jail and fines of one hundred dollars plus costs. The two ringleaders and chief attackers, W. R. Vinson and Kenneth Adams (a member of the board of directors of the Anniston Citizens Council) were later convicted of assault with intent to commit murder.

The judge who sentenced the four in the first trial complimented Cole for his handling of the situation. The mayor of Birmingham had been at Cole's show, and while Cole had been recovering from his shock over the attack, had sent a representative backstage with an apology. Support for Cole came from a variety of sources—newspaper people, disc jockeys, even a police chief in Charlotte, North Carolina. Back in Hollywood, Frank Sinatra spoke out against Cole's attackers, Geri Branton recalls. Cole believed he had behaved correctly. Privately, he was angry and frightened, but he saw no point in making an issue of the attack. Before leaving Birmingham, he told reporters that he was not "mad with anyone" in the South. "The ovation they gave me was really wonderful," he said, referring to the white audience's reaction to his return to the stage after the attack. "These people were trying to let me know they do not condone such actions. . . . I just hope I can get back to Alabama again soon to sing. I know I have many friends in the state, and I believe in them." Despite Carl Carruthers's advice to the contrary, Cole canceled only three engagements: Greenville, South Carolina, Charlotte and Raleigh, North Carolina. After playing for a week in Chicago, he resumed the tour and completed it without further incident.

Geri Branton met Nat at the airport when he returned from the Southern tour, and she was furious with him. His statement to reporters that he was not "mad with anyone" in the South still rankled. "I said,

'*You're* not made with anybody! I'm mad with *you*.'" She wasn't alone. Many blacks in the show business community felt that Cole should not have performed for segregated audiences in the first place. So did the black press. The *Baltimore Afro-American* charged that he was "kneeling before the throne of Jim Crow." The white press did its part. The *New York Post,* considered a liberal paper at the time, headlined a page two story "Cole Says He Won't Join the NAACP" and reported that Cole had pointedly refused an appeal from the NAACP to join in its fight against racism. Cole wired the NAACP that the story was untrue and sent a copy of his wire to the *Post,* which ran it under a tiny headline on page twenty.

Thurgood Marshall, then chief counsel for the NAACP, remarked that all Cole needed to complete his role as an Uncle Tom was a banjo. Several Harlem nightclubs took his records out of their jukeboxes. Nat was stung by this criticism, particularly by the charge that he was an Uncle Tom. But he maintained that he had behaved in the way that was best for him. "Those people, segregated or not, are still record fans," he told reporters. "They can't overpower the law of the South, and I can't come in on a one-night stand and overpower the law. The whites come to applaud a Negro performer like the colored do. When you've got the respect of white and colored, you can erase a lot of things. . . . I can help ease the tension by gaining the respect of both races all over the country."

It took some time for the controversy to die down, and Cole found himself in a defensive position, especially as regards the NAACP; he had to cite many times his long-standing support of that organization. As an example, here is a letter he wrote to *Down Beat* in May 1956:

Detroit, Mich.

To the Editor:

I have been quite concerned over reports appearing in newspapers which purport to represent my views on Jim Crow and discrimination. These reports also attributed to me statements I was supposed to have made regarding the NAACP and its activities.

First of all, I would like to say that I am, have been and will continue to be dedicated to the complete elimination of all forms of discrimination, segregation and bigotry. There is only one position in this matter and that is the right one: Full equality for all people, regardless of race, creed or religion.

This has been my position all along, and contrary to any published reports, it remains my position. I have fought, in what I considered an effective manner, against the evil of race bigotry through the years. I had hoped that through the medium of my music I had made many new friends and changed many opinions regarding racial equality. I have always been of the opinion that by living equality, living as a full American dedicated to the democratic principle, that [I] was helping fight bigotry by example much as the NAACP and other organizations have fought through the courts.

I do not want to be defensive about my position. I stand on my record. I have always supported the NAACP and other organizations fighting segregation and discrimination. Only last November I played a benefit for the Las Vegas Branch NAACP. Roy Wilkins has in his files my written offer to help in the NAACP program in whatever manner I can. I have in my personal records cancelled checks of my contributions to several NAACP chapters, as well as to the Montgomery bus boycott.

Since it is obvious that those who are opposed to equality and dignity of all men have used the unfortunate Birmingham incident as a weapon against the NAACP, against me, and against the fight for first class citizenship, *I am today subscribing to the NAACP as a life member* [emphasis added].

I sincerely hope, that in a small manner, this will set the record straight and help bring closer the day when bigotry and discrimination are things of the past, wherever they exist.

Nat (King) Cole

For a whole complex of reasons, Nat Cole could never be a militant. As a youngster he had accepted rather than fought against the idea that his black skin made him somehow inferior; and this attitude had followed him into adulthood. He felt that light-skinned blacks like Geri Branton did not really understand. She recalls, "He said to me one time, 'You think you're black and militant, but you don't know how it feels.' That's when he told me about the time on the bus in Chicago when the light-skinned woman said, 'You are black and you stink and you can never wash it off.'" His life with Maria, the feeling that lighter was better, that lighter meant more education and better diction and better taste in clothes, could only have further underscored his belief.

His own feelings about race aside, Cole was basically apolitical. He hadn't flirted with leftist causes as some of his fellow entertainers had; thus he was never blacklisted during the "Red Scare" of the early 1950s as they were. While no Negro could be entirely apolitical and while Cole resented the racism that made it necessary for him always to be alert and aware of his position in a world in which whites dominated, he could see little gain in trying to fight back on principle.

Being outspoken on racial matters would also have hurt his career, and he had worked too hard for success to jeopardize it. He would do benefit performances for civil rights causes and pursue his private civil rights battles against segregated neighborhoods, hotels, and Las Vegas casinos, but he was not about to go out on the hustings or call his people to arms. He was not that kind of man. As Maria Cole said in her autobiography of her husband, "Nat sincerely believed in the inherent good and kindness of man, that good did indeed eventually triumph over evil, and in the Christian ethic of turning the other cheek."

Whether Cole had originally come to this philosophy as an unconscious self-defense mechanism, it was still sincere and to be respected. Militant as she was and angry as she got at him, Geri Branton still has awe in her voice when she speaks of his character: "He was one of my favorite human beings of all time. I was fortunate to know him. He was the most unhating person I've ever known. He'd say, 'Geri, never allow yourself to hate a human being. Hate the system for what it's done to that person.' That advice has been very useful to me."

Nat did take a quite revolutionary step around that time. He hired Leo Branton as his attorney. By this time Geri and Fayard Nicholas had divorced and Geri had married Leo Branton. "We were close friends and had discussed Leo's representing Nat quite often," says Geri, "so it fell into place quite naturally." Except that it was not at all natural for black lawyers to represent black entertainers. White lawyers and agents were in the habit of warning black entertainers that hiring black attorneys would harm their careers, and, according to Geri Branton, Carlos Gastel was no exception. But Leo Branton had excellent credentials. "Leo took special courses and was truly prepared," says Geri. Nat hired Leo Branton, who subsequently handled Jimi Hendrix's estate, among many others. "Nat was happy to be a trailblazer," says Geri. If Thurgood Marshall *et al.* were aware of this forward-looking step on the road to racial solidarity by Cole, they didn't mention it publicly.

Cole finally got his own television series that fall. Had he spoken out against Southern racism a few months earlier, he might have been passed over yet again.

He had wanted to be in television since its beginnings, but the fact of his race had kept him off the home screen for years.

There had been few blacks on television. Bob Howard had a series called "Sing It Again" in the late forties, but it was soon canceled for lack of sponsorship. Occasionally, a black appeared in a special—Sidney Poitier in Robert Alan Aurthur's "A Man Is Ten Feet Tall," Ossie Davis in "The Emperor Jones," Marian Anderson in "See It Now." Only one black appeared regularly on television—Eddie "Rochester" Anderson, the comic servant on the "Jack Benny Show." Blacks did not fit the image that television wanted to present to America, and that included even blacks who were immensely popular in other fields of entertainment.

Even with record stardom, Cole had to be content with guest spots on variety shows. Maria says that being on television regularly—having a show of his own—was for him a way to prove himself, but for a long time no one was willing to let him try. His representatives put out the word that he was available, even eager, to have a show, but with no results. Finally, Cole could take it no longer. He informed Carlos Gastel and his booking agency, General Artists Corporation, that if they didn't make a television deal, he would not renew his contract with them. When in the spring of 1956 Frankie Carlyle canceled his contract for his show with NBC, Cole was given his opportunity at last. "The Frankie Carlyle Show" was a mere fifteen minutes one afternoon a week, but Nat Cole was willing to take any opportunity to get his foot in TV's door.

There wasn't much money available for "The Nat 'King' Cole Show," which aired for the first time in the fall of 1956. NBC put the show on the air without a sponsor, hoping that Cole's performance on television would attract advertisers. Cole had a band backing him up, the musicians working for scale, but there was little or nothing left over for production. Cole's comparatively small salary went back into production costs, and since he had to rearrange his performance schedule so as to be in New

York or Hollywood or some other major city with facilities to do telecasts for a certain number of weeks, he was forced to make further financial sacrifices. He believed these sacrifices to be worthwhile, however, if he could have the opportunity to reach the wider audience television provided.

By the summer of 1957 "The Nat 'King' Cole Show" had increased its audience rating by 45 percent and its share of audience by 29 percent, and although it still had no major sponsorship NBC gambled on expanding it to a half-hour summer variety show in prime time (Tuesdays 10–10:30 P.M. EDT). A number of top musical stars guested on the show, working for scale—Peggy Lee, Ella Fitzgerald, Kay Starr, the Mills Brothers, and even Harry Belafonte, whose fee for television appearances was so high that most shows couldn't afford him. But it was still "The Nat 'King' Cole Show," and as such it still didn't attract major advertisers, even when the advertisers were offered drastically reduced rates. Major sponsors explained that they had to worry about the South, though such an argument had a hollow ring to it. Few stations in the South ever carried the show, and thus the majority of Southerners would never have the opportunity to associate a product with Nat King Cole. Far more worrisome for the major sponsors was the less overt but no less commercially deadly racism in the North.

When fall came, NBC continued to carry the show, moving it to Tuesdays 7:30–8:00 P.M. One reason it could stay on the air was that major artists were still willing to work for scale—a couple of hundred dollars—and Cole himself was working for fifteen hundred dollars when his usual fee for television guest appearance was seventy-five hundred dollars. But after a time NBC was unwilling to carry the show even at a relatively small loss. When they moved the show to Saturdays 7 P.M., a slot known in the industry as "cowboy time," Carlos Gastel told the network to forget it. The last "Nat 'King' Cole Show" aired in December 1957; in one format or another it had run for a total of sixty weeks, and Cole was left poorer and embittered by the experience. He didn't blame show business, he blamed advertisers. "Sponsors don't have any guts," he said. "Madison Avenue is afraid of the dark." It took him several years to get over what he regarded as an affront to his talent and professionalism.

What helped him to do so was his feeling that in the long run, regular exposure on television wasn't good for singers: They became overexposed, and their record sales, as well as demand for concert appearances, suffered. He cited as examples of TV overexposure such stars as Dinah Shore and Perry Como. In dealing with his disappointment in this way, he may have taken a cue from his wife and put the best face on a bad situation.

Fortunately the opportunity to appear in a movie came along at just about the time he left television. He'd wanted to be in films even more than he'd wanted to be on television, and in 1957 he was cast as a French foreign legionnaire in *China Gate.* It was the story of the struggle for control of Indochina told through the eyes of a small band of legionnaires who are trying to reach a hidden communist munitions dump. Cole's being cast as one of the legionnaires, along with Gene Barry, Lee Van Cleef, and others, was a great step beyond his earlier roles in major films, in which he was mere decoration. While some critics said he overacted in *China Gate,* others believed he handled his dual assignment of straight role plus singing the title song well. Hollywood was still willing to bet its money on him. He was, after all, a big-name singing star, and Hollywood didn't see why it couldn't cash in on his success.

St. Louis Blues was his next picture and his first starring vehicle other than the twenty-minute biographical film in which he had played himself. The highly fictionalized biography of black jazz composer W. C. Handy had a star-studded cast including Cole as Handy, Eartha Kitt, Cab Calloway, Pearl Bailey, Ruby Dee, Juano Hernandez, Mahalia Jackson, and Ella Fitzgerald.

Of the group, only Bailey had proved to have the ability to go from stage to screen successfully. The others were cast not because of their acting ability but for their stardom in other media; but they were game to try.

Cole worked very hard to become W. C. Handy in that film, worked to bring to the role his own struggles as a jazz musician in the early days. When principal filming was completed, he was enthusiastic about the picture: "It's one of the biggest movies in film history," he told columnist Joe Hyams, "and it's coming out at a good time, when movie business generally is off. It will give us a good test to see if the public will buy an all-Negro film. If this picture makes money, you can bet there will be plenty more."

The road for blacks in Hollywood films had been a rocky one. Except for the few all-black films they released during the war years, like *Stormy Weather* and *Cabin in the Sky,* the major studios had offered few important or dignified roles to blacks. Beginning in the mid-1940s, blacks hadn't been offered even stereotypical roles. In response to protests from the NAACP and other groups that blacks were never portrayed in Hollywood films as real people, that they were presented only as stereotypes, the studios had simply eliminated most black parts. Black entertainers often got more work in films than black dramatic actors and actresses, doing specialty numbers that weren't integral to the plot and were thus easily cut by Southern censors. In fact, when in the early 1950s Hollywood began to produce black films again, entertainers were more likely than dramatic actors to star in these films. Lionel Hampton, Louis Armstrong, Ella Fitzgerald, Eartha Kitt, and Pearl Bailey were among these entertainers turned actors, in addition to Nat Cole. Few were able to make the transition successfully.

Eartha Kitt starred with Cole in *St. Louis Blues.* She came off, according to Donald Bogle in his book *Toms, Coons, Mulattos, Mammies and Bucks,* as "a terribly affected and studied actress with too many self-conscious kinks and quirks ... [and] ... an underlying bitchiness that antagonized filmgoers." Mahalia Jackson and Pearl Bailey were treated more generously, but their performances weren't enough to save the film. According to Bogle, Nat Cole's performance was the greatest disappointment: "Thin and anemic and much too suave and courteous, Cole seemed out of place, and it was apparent that he lacked the strength and range to carry the picture."

Critics at the time were not so hard on him. The *Los Angeles Herald Examiner* called his performance a fine one, laced with dignity and charm; the critic for *Variety* blamed the script, not Cole, for failing to capture Handy. Still, that was Cole's last starring role. It may well be that his lifetime of holding his true feelings in check is what prevented him from being able to handle a leading role and doomed him to supporting roles thereafter. In *The Night of the Quarter Moon,* he played Julie

London's beleaguered uncle in a film in which a wealthy San Franciscan (John Drew Barrymore) unwittingly marries a quadroon (London) and scandalizes himself and his family when her racial heritage is revealed. It was another version of the hackneyed "tragic mulatto" story; and it should be pointed out that even if Nat had proved a gifted actor Hollywood could have offered him few roles commensurate with his talents. Whether the main problem was Nat's acting or a lack of vehicles for him, his dream of being a leading man in movies came to nothing.

So did his one attempt at musical theater, in 1960. *I'm with You,* a musical, was financed jointly by Cole and Capitol Records in what was a new venture for both. Cole, who put up half the $150,000 financing, had never before invested so heavily in anything. Capitol had never before backed a show in order to promote one of its own stars. Ordinarily record companies invested in shows in order to obtain rights to original cast albums. Dotty Wayne and Ray Rasch wrote the music, book, and lyrics for *I'm with You,* which opened in Denver on October 17 and was scheduled to wind up in Boston at the end of January before going on to Broadway in early February. It starred Cole and a new actress-singer named Barbara McNair. Young Natalie Cole also had a small part. Unfortunately the show garnered such consistently poor reviews that it was forced to close in Detroit before making it to Boston and New York. Cole didn't try that genre again.

For Carol and Natalie Cole, the nicest thing about their father's comparatively brief career as a leading man was that, once again, he stayed put in Los Angeles for a while. Carol was in high school by then and a little too wild in her mother's opinion. She had attended nearby John Burroughs Junior High School only briefly, then transferred to Immaculate Heart High School, where, she says, "I would get the proper discipline—and you know there are no boys in Catholic school." Like any other self-respecting teenager, Carol was enamored of rock 'n' roll, and she remembers that her father differed from most self-respecting parents in that he appreciated this music. She was old enough by this time to understand her father as a musician, and she feels that being with him gave her "my love for musicians and my understanding of what they're about. They're in the upper echelon of crazies—it's fabulous, and it's also very difficult. I always feel that he missed a lot or gave up a lot when he became a pop star, a vocalist. His first love and his last love was the musician in him, the keyboard artist."

For Cole, however, it was impossible to go back to being a keyboard artist. He couldn't look back. And since TV and Hollywood were beyond his reach, for one reason or another he was forced to remain a pop artist—making records and giving concerts. Within those comparatively narrow confines, he continued to expand as much as he could. In 1958 he turned his attention to the Latin market, a market that Carlos Gastel had been watching for some time and in which Gastel, having been born in Latin America, would have had a personal interest. Aware that Cole's records had sold well in Latin America over the years, Gastel suggested a short tour in Cuba.

At that time Cuba, particularly Havana, was an American play-ground—a favorite stop for tourists with its casinos and floor shows and resort hotels. At Havana's Tropicana club, Cole sang in English and was perfectly well understood by the majority of the club's patrons. But he knew that many Cubans were fans of his, and when he met some native musicians he began to feel that the least he could do was learn Spanish. He expressed his feelings in "Music—The Universal Language," a short article in the *Hollywood Reporter*: "When you say 'thank you' to a foreigner, it's more gracious to say it in his language, not yours." He cut an album of songs in Spanish that year. To prepare for *Cole Español,* he studied with Val Valentine, his engineer at Capitol Records and a Spaniard. Armando Romeu, Jr., a Cuban conductor, led the orchestra that backed him on the album. Capitol promoted the album heavily in Spanish-speaking countries, and in 1959 Cole went on his first major Latin American tour, accompanied not only by Maria but also by Carol and Natalie.

The six-week tour was not officially sponsored by the U.S. Depart-ment of State, but it had the blessing of that department. Cole proved to be an excellent goodwill ambassador. His fans were so numerous that wherever he went he had to be protected from admiring crowds by crash-helmeted police. In Argentina he was able to have enough contact with ordinary Argentinians to conclude that "a lot of the poor people still like Perón." In Caracas he gave a benefit concert for the Catholic Boys

Clubs, a concert that was coordinated by the U.S. ambassador to Venezuela and the Venezuelan government.

Carol was about fourteen by then, Natalie about nine. Nat hadn't given up the desire to have a son, but Maria, after her miscarriage several years before, hadn't conceived again. As she explained in her biography of Nat, the two decided that the simplest and surest way to have a son was to adopt one. Initially they considered adopting a Korean interracial baby fathered by a black American serviceman. The plight of such children was of great concern to Nat, who while in Germany in 1960 would join Cause, a German organization backed by former American boxer Al Hoosman that helped finance the education of 100,000 black and white illegitimate children fathered and forgotten by American servicemen in Germany. They had read that the children of both white and black servicemen would be discriminated against in Korean society and that half-Negro children would have an especially hard time. But eventually the Coles decided that there were enough full-blooded American black babies in need of homes. They went to the Children's Home Society of California.

In an article in *Ebony* about the child they adopted, Nat wrote, "Ironically enough, we applied the same month (last February) that our son was born." In July they were invited to the agency to see a five-and-a-half-month-old infant. Practically the moment he saw the child, Cole decided he was the son they'd been waiting for. Allowing Carol and Natalie to play with him for an hour or so at the agency was a mere formality. Maria wrote in her book that it was only after they'd taken the child home that it occurred to her that she hadn't asked a thing about him. She needn't have worried. He was healthy, bright, and so similar to Natalie in skin tone and in the shape of his eyes that most people assumed that the boy was Nat's and Maria's biological son.

It was Maria's idea to name the little boy Nat Kelly Cole. Nat had been born on Saint Patrick's day, so Kelly was a fitting name, and he would have the same initials as his father. He was christened at L.A.'s Saint James Episcopal Church, and Leo and Geri Branton were his godparents.

Nat and Maria never kept from Kelly the fact that he was adopted. "They told me before I really had any idea what it meant," he says. "They made it sound like something special. They said, 'You were special. We didn't have to have you, we chose you.' In fact, being somewhat of a little brat as a kid, I used to lord it over my younger sisters." For Nat, Kelly was a dream come true, and he spent as much time as he could with him. About a month after Kelly's arrival, Cole had to go on an Eastern tour. He told *Ebony,* "I took one look at him in his crib and told Maria that I couldn't leave him. He went to Chicago and New York with us. We had a baby crib and all the accessories, and we hired a regular nurse to take care of him. He took to it like a duck takes to water. He especially enjoyed New York and long walks in Central Park."

Cole also said that before making the decision to adopt his son, he knew "that I would have to cut down on my personal appearances. Cookie and Sweetie are used to my hectic schedule, but I had to consider the effect it would have on a growing boy. Of course, we have a nurse and housekeeper, but in the formative years a man should be around the house to help bring up his own child."

That he hadn't been around much to help bring up Cookie and Sweetie probably didn't even occur to him when he made those statements. He was thinking of his little boy not of his considerably older daughters. One wonders, however, what Carol and Natalie, who no doubt read the article in *Ebony,* thought. They weren't jealous of young Kelly, but their tenuous hold on a special place in their father's heart must have been threatened.

The only time Kelly disappointed his father, according to Maria, was when he didn't take to baseball. Cole expected his son to love the game as he did, and by the age of fourteen months Kelly had three baseball uniforms, three bats, and a catcher's mask. But Kelly refused to play baseball. He may have done so out of jealousy toward the activity that so frequently took his father away from the home. Maria reported in her book that one time when she and Nat were at a game and Kelly was home with his Aunt Barba listening to the game on radio, the youngster demanded, "Come on *anybody* and get a hit so my mommy and daddy can come home."

As so often happens to people who try to have children and, failing to do so, adopt, Maria became pregnant the year following Kelly's adoption. She states in her book that she was not pleased. She was close to forty years old, her eldest daughter was in high school, she had been a mother for some twelve years already and now faced another twenty-two years of motherhood. The prospect of caring for another infant was difficult enough to adjust to; then, a week before her due date, she learned that she was carrying twins. Nat was scheduled for a trip to Canada, and she feared that he wouldn't even be around when the babies were born. He assured her that he would be with her, and he was.

Complications hampered delivery of the twins, and for an anxious time all three lives hung in the balance. Informed of the problems, Cole instructed Maria's doctors to save her life. Geri Branton, who was also at the Catholic hospital, felt constrained to remind the nurses that while it was Catholic belief that the child's life came first, Maria Cole was not Catholic. Fortunately both mother and children came through. The twins were girls, and again Maria apologized to her husband for not having boys. Again, Nat assured her that all he cared about was their health and hers. She says that her usually undemonstrative husband was "completely uninhibited in his expression of love for me" at this time, but he still went to Canada as planned, and she suffered severe postpartum depression during his absence.

Nat named one of the twins Casey, after Casey Stengel, perhaps in the hope that she would develop the interest in baseball that young Kelly lacked. Songwriter Johnny Burke named the other little girl Timolin. Kelly coped with the arrival of the babies by assuring himself that he was special because his parents had chosen him, and the two older girls played at being mothers to the twins, just as they did with Kelly.

Carol made her debut that year, 1961, presented to Los Angeles society by the city's Links chapter, a national black women's sorority, at a debutantes' ball at the Beverly Hilton Hotel. That same evening President John F. Kennedy was honored at a dinner given at the Hollywood Palladium, and Cole had been invited to attend and perform. He went to the dinner and made his appearance on the dais with the president, then, explaining to Kennedy that he had to leave in order to present his daughter at the debutantes' ball, rushed to the Hilton. Kennedy, who admired Cole and who no doubt also saw a chance to score points with L.A.'s black society, later made a surprise appearance at the ball, greeting all the debutantes and giving special attention to Carol. He told the group,

"Nat sang at our dinner tonight, so I thought I'd reciprocate. I'm grateful to you girls for letting an itinerant president come and visit your party."

It isn't every young girl who has a president in attendance at her debut, but then Cookie Cole wasn't just any young girl. She was Nat King Cole's eldest daughter, and she had grown up with a socioeconomic security, if not an emotional security, that is to be envied. The Cole papers at the University of Southern California include photographs of one of her birthday parties, when she was about seven. None of the other little children in the photograph is black. There is also a photograph of her and her father on her seventeenth birthday; Cole escorted her to the premiere of *Breakfast at Tiffany's*. *Ebony* featured her debut at the Links Cotillion, covering "a day in the life of a debutante" and beginning at the Cole home at 4 A.M. The Cole children knew neither poverty nor the overt racism experienced by less-sheltered black youngsters. They lived a comparatively rarified existence, one that many other blacks, not to mention whites, resented. Maria Cole didn't seem to display a great deal of concern about how anyone else felt; she simply wanted the best for herself and her family. "A lot of people were alienated because they thought she was living too grand to be black," says Kelly Cole. "They thought it was an affectation, but it really wasn't an affectation with her. It was her New England formality that alienated people. Black people really have a chip on their shoulder about other black people succeeding. They tried to make her feel guilty, but she wouldn't accept it."

10

Death
of a
King

THE early sixties were a time when successful blacks were particularly susceptible to guilt feelings. In 1960 young blacks in the South had demonstrated how ineffective the traditional accommodation to racism was compared to direct-action tactics. Black students at North Carolina Agricultural and Technical College in Greensboro had sat in at a local Woolworth's luncheonette, and the student civil rights movement had spread like wildfire across the South. Older civil rights leaders, among them Martin Luther King, Jr., who had become prominent in the course of the successful bus boycott in Montgomery, Alabama, four years earlier, were caught unawares by the students' actions and had hastily moved to include the youngsters within the framework of the established, though still incipient, movement. While remaining true to the principles of nonviolence that men like King espoused, the students had speeded up things, forcing older activists to play catch-up. The epithet Uncle Tom was not yet being bandied about

153

thoughtlessly, but it was on a lot of people's minds, including the minds of people who thought it just might apply to them. Some highly successful and visible blacks, including some in the entertainment business, felt guilty about not having done more to break down the racial barriers in their country but were too afraid of being rejected by the young activists if they tried, now, to step into the fray. Others, like Nat Cole, seem not to have felt any sense of guilt. In spite of the fact that he'd been called an Uncle Tom by Thurgood Marshall Cole believed he'd done what he had to do, and while he increased the number of benefit performances he gave on behalf of civil rights organizations, he confined his activity to work "within the system."

In the spring of 1960 Cole and Harry Belafonte formed a partnership aimed at increasing black participation in television and movies. Cole-Belafonte Enterprises (they flipped a coin to decide whose name would come first) would produce films and television specials but not necessarily star in them. "We want others to get into star position," Cole explained to a *New York Herald Tribune* reporter. Their chief goal was to break down barriers for black performers. "Between us," Cole said, "we have helped open up doors in motion pictures and television. But the old stereotype is being perpetuated. This we hope to discourage. We hope to encourage more faithful portrayals of the American Negro, more opportunities. There are lots of ways Negroes can be used in films without making controversial or message pictures." Cole didn't anticipate too many problems getting financial backing for their projects. "The Negro performer has risen in stature," he explained. "He is meeting with nationwide acceptance on his own merits." The partnership and the company, however, were short-lived. Cole cited "artistic disagreements," but one suspects there was more to the failure of the partnership than that. Cole's optimism notwithstanding, America was still not ready to accept black entertainers, even highly successful ones, on their own terms. Still, Cole kept trying. The following year, he formed Kell-Cole Productions, named after his son, Kelly, to do the same things he had hoped to do in association with Belafonte.

American television was still largely closed to blacks. The Canadian Broadcasting Corporation (CBC) produced specials starring American blacks several years before American networks did, among them Lena

Horne's first TV special, produced by Harry Belafonte, in 1968. Seven years before that, in 1961, Canadian TV aired a Nat King Cole special produced by Kell-Cole Productions that was so well received that an American television network expressed interest in buying it. The show was called *Wild Is Love* after a successful Cole record album that had been released in 1960. "It was a concept album," says Kelly Cole, "with a story line throughout, and in a way you might say the special was the first popular music video. They'd sold it to American television and had a sponsor for it." But negotiations ran into a snag over the ending of one number. "Larry Kert, a Canadian guy who was in *West Side Story* and *Side by Side by Sondheim* sang a duet with Dad," says Kelly. "At the end of it, Dad puts his arm around him and they walk offstage. Well, they got a telegram saying the only way the sponsor would take the show was if that segment—the approximately three and a half seconds when two men, a white and a black, had physical contact—was cut. Stan Harris [of Kell-Cole Productions] says he wishes he'd kept that telegram. They declined to cut the segment." Not until 1964 did that special air on American television, and then only on a local television station in New York, WPIX.

Nor was Cole any more successful in films, despite his popularity as a singer and recording artist. After the ill-fated *St. Louis Blues* and *Night of the Quarter Moon*, he had only one other role in a movie, a musical role that was reminiscent of his roles in the late 1930s and 1940s—he played a singing troubadour in *Cat Ballou*.

Disappointed as he was over his failure to break down the racial barriers in television and films, Nat could always take comfort in his ability to return to the club or concert stage and the recording studio with relatively undiminished popularity. He played only extended engagements now—usually four weeks. The only one-night stands he played were on tours abroad, which included another tour of Europe with a big band led by Quincy Jones in 1960 and his first tour in Japan in 1962.

While in Europe he unwittingly got into a flap with his old friend Norman Granz, who had arranged the tour. Interviewed in Frankfurt, Germany, by Hazel Guild of *Variety*, Cole criticized rock 'n' roll, blamed record companies for propping it up through payola, and predicted that television would kill rock and roll: "Jazz in the U.S. is at the bottom of the commercial barrel. It doesn't draw enough business, and that's why rock and roll came into being. That isn't a sign that it's any good—but there is a buying public for it. . . . Television is an even more ruthless business [than the payola-scandalized record industry]. It's the beatniks with the long hair and dark glasses and the kids who like rock and roll. And they aren't the people who buy the mass-consumption articles advertised on television. To get the most people to watch, and to buy, they'll have to eliminate rock and roll."

So much for Cole's predictive powers, though, perhaps more than anything else, these statements about rock and roll belie his own, killing, experience with the power of television and its advertisers.

The following week, *Variety* carried a letter from Norman Granz rebutting Cole. He was "talking through his hat" when he said that jazz was at the bottom of the commercial barrel in the United States, wrote Granz. "Nat should know better because jazz in every conceivable form is bigger than ever, being used not only in concerts but on films, on television, and obviously on records. Let him check the sales of Brubeck and Garner on Columbia and Ella Fitzgerald on Verve. And he need only to look at the jazz concert grosses to know how well they're doing."

Ironically, Granz himself was no longer based in the United States, or on the U.S. jazz scene. In 1959 he had moved to Geneva, Switzerland. In 1960 he had sold Verve Records to MGM. He returned to his native country only rarely, for a few days on business involving singer Ella Fitzgerald and jazz pianist Oscar Peterson, both of whom he still managed. He devoted most of his time to presenting major American artists to European audiences, not only jazz artists like Duke Ellington, Ray Charles, and Count Basie but nonjazz attractions like Richie Havens and the Mothers of Invention. In 1972 he complained to music critic Leonard Feather that it was impossible to do "a nice, quiet inexpensive jazz concert" in the United States and that there was more "stability" in Europe. Thus, Nat's predictions about jazz were not so far off the mark.

As a highly successful pop vocalist, Nat had no trouble getting extended engagements and in getting favorable contractual terms. While Maria had frequently traveled with him, even when he was playing a lot of one-nighters, it was now easier to take the children along. Kelly remembers traveling with his parents frequently. The twins were often

taken along, and Carol and Natalie went, too, when their school schedules permitted. While nightclub critics must have found themselves at a
loss for fresh ways to describe his voice, his style of presentation, and his
music, they never expressed boredom. Cole's performances were as
consistently well received as his records were consistently bought.
Younger singers studied him, trying to find the secret of his professional
longevity; Ray Charles openly admitted copying him. After twenty-five
years in the business, Nat King Cole was still the king.

The year 1962 marked the twenty-fifth anniversary of Cole's founding
of his trio, and in August Capitol Records and the Los Angeles chapter of
the Urban League sponsored a tribute to him. The nine-hundred-seat
Embassy Room of the Ambassador Hotel was filled to overflowing with
guests who came to honor Cole, among them Doris Day, Art Linkletter,
Jerry Lewis, Joe Louis, Groucho Marx, Mickey Rooney, Robert Stack,
Connie Stevens, Gene Barry, and Ed Wynn. Edie Adams organized the
entertainment. Jaye P. Morgan, Patti Page, Rosemary Clooney, and Gary
Crosby sang songs with special lyrics by Sammy Cahn and Jimmy
Van Heusen. Mahalia Jackson sang a spirited rendition of "Joshua." Earl
"Fatha" Hines recalled the early days in Chicago when Cole was just
starting out. Dick Gregory made some biting comments about racial
bigotry, and so did Dick Shawn. Steve Allen acted as master of ceremo-
nies. Just a few hours before the tribute to Cole, the Hollywood community had been stunned by the news of Marilyn Monroe's suicide. Toward
the end of the evening Allen mentioned Monroe's death and remarked
that the tribute to Cole was a heartwarming contrast, for in Cole's case
people had not waited until it was too late to demonstrate their affection.
Allen had no way of knowing how prophetic his statements would prove
to be.

Musical tastes had changed by the early 1960s. Rock 'n' roll, which owed
so much to black performers like Chuck Berry but which did not become
widely popular until white artists took it up in the mid-fifties, was still in
ascendance with no end in sight. A small company in Detroit called
Hitsville USA (later to be renamed Motown) had found a winning
combination of rock, gospel, and "ghetto sound" and in 1962 produced
five hit records by local groups called the Contours and the Marvellettes

and by an individual named Mary Wells. The major record-buying audience had also changed; the consumers who made hits of "Please Mr. Postman" and "You Beat Me to the Punch" were younger, on the average, than those who had demanded "The Christmas Song" and "Nature Boy" in unprecedented numbers. Nat Cole faced these changes in taste and audience with a certain ambivalence.

On the one hand, he regretted the idea of being a sort of venerable institution in his early forties, felt rather in limbo—his records no longer made the Top Ten, but they were often in the Top Twenty. As if to remind his audiences that his particular sound was different from and had been around much longer than the newer material, he began to include in his act a song called "Mr. Cole Won't Rock 'n' Roll." It also bothered him that comparatively few people knew him as anything but a singer; he brushed up on his piano playing and began to include a good fifteen minutes of straight playing in his live performances. On the other hand, he understood and appreciated the new music and had no desire to crusade against it. "He'd come in and listen to my Smokey Robinson records," says Carol, who graduated from high school in 1962. "That 'Mr. Cole Won't Rock 'n' Roll' business was media stuff. I felt that he was always open to whatever was going on and really embraced a lot of it." Some of Cole's own recordings from that period were viewed by some critics as attempts to reach an audience for whom snapping one's fingers to a beat was more important than pondering the meaning of a lyric. "Those Lazy-Hazy-Crazy Days of Summer" and "Ramblin' Rose" were cited by many critics as unabashed corn.

Cole was merely adjusting to changes in the market. Another change that had come about by the early 1960s concerned the stages where entertainment was presented: The number of glamorous nightclubs and hotel entertainment rooms was shrinking. People just didn't dress up and go out to such places anymore unless they were in Las Vegas or Lake Tahoe. Even New York and Los Angeles had fewer stages of that type. Concerts in huge arenas like Madison Square Garden, Radio City Music Hall, and the Hollywood Bowl were the most popular form of live entertainment. Thus, in 1962, Cole, in association with Ike Jones of Kell-Cole Productions, created a concert show called *Sights and Sounds* that featured Cole and a group of young singers and dancers called the Merry Young Souls. Cole took the show on the road for six weeks in 1962 and was sufficiently pleased with its success to take it out on the road again in 1963 and 1964. In the three years the show ran, it played in more than one hundred cities across the country, including cities in Kentucky, Maryland, and Tennessee, his first performances in the South since the 1956 tour.

The fact that his integrated group of singers and dancers were allowed to perform on Southern stages was proof to Cole that racial relations could change and that the best tactic for promoting change was a professionalism that invited the respect of one's fellow human beings, whatever their color.

Cole enjoyed the change of pace that "Sights and Sounds" represented for him. In her book Maria quotes him as saying, "I played nightclubs for a long while, and I sort of need the change mentally. Besides, I wanted to create a new image, so I'm performing before a vast new audience. They say only 40 percent of the people attend nightclubs. So, if I play New York City, I'm not performing for the people of New York, I'm playing for those comparative few who go to the Copacabana. Also, there are kids who can't go to nightclubs, but who can and do come to concerts." Besides injecting some freshness into his own performing routine, Cole's creation of "Sights and Sounds" was good business.

"Listen," he told a British interviewer in 1963. "I'm a business man. I work for business people. The kind of thing they say is: Now we've sold a lot of records, let's sell some more. I try to appease both sides but it's tough. The jazz people think that everybody outside them is square. Oh God, they say, he's going commercial. . . ." And to another interviewer he explained, "As soon as you start to make money in the popular field they scream about how good you were in the good old days and what a bum you are now. Well, the good old days were good on the ear, but hard on the pocket."

Cole made a major change in his business relationships in 1963. He and Carlos Gastel dissolved their twenty-year association, one of the most mutually profitable in the entertainment industry. Although the partnership ended officially on December 31, 1963, the two made the formal announcement on August 1. "Due to the fact that I now have my own

Kell-Cole Co., equipped to handle many of the functions of the personal manager, I no longer require outside representation in that field of activity," read Cole's statement. The statement added that Kell-Cole had arranged for Gastel to stay on as a special executive adviser to the company but did not specify his duties. Kell-Cole Productions at this time consisted of Cole, attorney Leo Branton, and Ike Jones, producer of Cole's stage shows.

According to the official statements, Cole and Gastel parted amicably, but according to Geri Branton, wife of Leo Branton, the changeover was very difficult: "We were scared to death. Leo [felt] threatened." Gastel was hardly eager to give up his percentage of Cole's income, and he did not give it up without a fight. Then, too, blacks had been traditionally barred from positions of power in the representation of major black entertainers. Branton was one of the first black entertainment lawyers. "It was so difficult to get black people to go to black lawyers," says Geri Branton. "Leo is a very efficient, very capable man. He pulled Nat out of the morass, straightened out his taxes, made sound investments. Leo put them on a strict budget."

Cole now talked more about his business dealings to interviewers. Perhaps he wished to stress that there was nother dimension to him than that of singer. Perhaps he was simply talking about what was on his mind; he may have been hoping that good investments would enable him to retire from the entertainment business. With some frequency interviewers reported, and were presumably informed by Cole, that under the aegis of Leo Branton he had made a number of investments. He was a partner in the sponsorship of a middleweight fighter named Gene Johns who he quickly decided wasn't "hungry" enough. He was sponsoring a young singer named Frank D'Rome. He was part owner of a paper cup manufacturing concern in Puerto Rico. He was president of Kell-Cole Productions. On hearing of these various ventures, British columnist David Griffiths speculated, "My guess is that Nat will milk the market as much as he can in the next year or two, and then concentrate more on business than on singing. Nat Cole, the millionaire businessman, will take over."

The columnist made that forecast on the occasion of Cole's arrival in London for his first British tour since 1954. He was accompanied onstage by Ted Heath and his orchestra, who had last toured with Cole in the American South in 1956; and by three musicians, including John Collins on guitar. Offstage, Cole was accompanied by Maria, Kelly, Natalie, and Carol. As Kelly recalls, the twins were too little to go.

Cole opened his tour at Finsbury Park Astoria in London on July 13, played at Hammersmith Odeon July 14, then played one-night stands in Glasgow, Leeds, Birmingham, Manchester, and Liverpool. In between he rehearsed and taped a BBC television special. Returning to London, he completed his fifteen-day tour, performing at the Lewisham Odeon and again at the Hammersmith Odeon. The tour was highly successful, and according to one reviewer that was because Cole managed to please all three of his "publics": "Teenagers prefer the Cole of the moment, who maintains his grip on the hit parade. . . . The teenagers received their ration of recent hits. . . . Romantics revelled as he sauntered about the stage, a man in a happy trance always leaning backwards as he sang purely and tenderly: 'To the End of the Earth,' 'The Song Is Ended,' and 'Hi Lili, Hi Lo.'" Aficionados of the Nat King Cole who'd traveled with a trio "shouted when [he] sat down to play the piano. A surprise to most of the audience who thought he had abandoned his old jazz ways. He played and sang 'It's Only a Paper Moon,' and thanks to the liquid guitar of John E. Collins, the old trio days were reborn.

"He tore off his supercharged 'Tea for Two,' throwing in a few tinkles from 'Surrey with the Fringe on Top.' He gave us 'Sweet Lorraine,' one of the few love songs which are both perfect and cheerful. And he brought all three parts of the audience together as he played and sang another song of the same rare breed: 'Let There Be Love.'"

While in Britain, Cole kept up with news of the civil rights movement back in his own country. The movement had grown steadily and so had its momentum. That year freedom riders had begun traveling into the South on interstate buses and on several occasions had been attacked by club-wielding white racists. In Glasgow Cole read that Marlon Brando, who had been outspoken in his support of the movement, planned to ride a "freedom bus" into the South. Reporters asked Cole what he planned to do on behalf of the movement. "I'm prepared to do my bit," he answered. But his "bit" did not include participation in a civil rights march in Washington in August in support of a civil rights bill proposed by

President John F. Kennedy. He had a singing engagement in Pittsburgh. He did say, however, that he thought the march was a good thing. Maria agreed, "as long as it is done in a dignified manner."

The Coles' political activism centered around work for the Democratic Party and particularly for the Kennedys, who made a point of seeking out prominent blacks, Lena Horne and writer James Baldwin among them. Maria served on the committee for a benefit performance of *PT 109* given in Los Angeles for the new Joseph P. Kennedy, Jr., Home for Retarded Children in Santa Monica. Cole went to Washington to sing at a Democratic fund-raising dinner and during the same visit accompanied Attorney General Robert F. Kennedy to a local high school to speak against dropping out of school. Hearing that Cole was in town, President Kennedy invited him to the White House, and Cole left with five pens, a pocketful of *PT 109* tie clasps, and an invitation from the president to Maria for a special tour of the White House.

Maria never had the opportunity to tour the Kennedy White House. A few months later the president was assassinated in Dallas. Among the Cole papers at USC is a letter from Lyndon B. Johnson expressing his appreciation of their condolence letter to him. The following January Cole was invited to Washington to entertain at a Senate Office Building luncheon sponsored by the Hollywood Museum to mark the seventieth anniversary of the first motion picture copyright. He accepted the invitation and also asked for an appointment with President Johnson, to whom he pledged his support and whom he found to be a "fine gentleman." Following President Kennedy, he said, was "like following a top act in show business—somebody, say, with a flair like Jolson—but every man has his own style."

One of Johnson's top priorities, as set forth in his first State of the Union Address, was to finish the work in the area of civil rights legislation that Kennedy had started. Cole applauded that commitment, but neither it nor the death of his beloved President Kennedy in a Southern city galvanized him to enter the civil rights crusade. Questions of his stand on civil rights issues had dogged him for several years already and would continue to do so until his death. By 1964 reporters noted that he displayed visible tension when they questioned him on integration. He never wavered in his stand: He was a professional entertainer not a

professional Negro. It was not enough for whites to accept black entertainers. "We can be something special, little dolls. We're no threat to
anybody. When people see us, they're relaxed, unworried. If Harry
Belafonte or Sammy Davis walks in someplace, then they will be recognized and concessions may be made. That's no good. Let a brilliant doctor
or lawyer or educator be recognized as a worthwhile man—then we'll be
doing something." His usual response was to say, "The first thing I'm
fighting for is individualism"; he would then decline to "mouth
platitudes."

Twenty years later a certain revisionist trend among thinking blacks
views Cole's position more generously. While the revisionists see the
militant civil rights movement and the black power movement that
followed as unavoidable, they do fault the more extreme standard bearers
for fostering destructive rather than constructive goals. They point to
Eldridge Cleaver, born-again Christian; Bobby Seale, a cookbook writer
in Philadelphia now; or Amiri Baraka, who has undergone several
political transformations since the 1960s, and ascribe to them much of the
blame for leading a legion of impressionable young people down the
garden path. In the revisionist view, so-called Uncle Toms like Nat Cole
were not such traitors after all. But in 1964 there were few blacks who
could or would defend him. His stand on civil rights was a very lonely
one.

He was lonely in his personal life as well. By 1964, Nat's and Maria's
seventeen-year marriage was under considerable strain, and had been for
some time. "There was no divorce going on or anything like that," says
Kelly Cole, "but they had stepped back and decided that they would
really have to evaluate their relationship before going on. That happens in
relationships after seventeen years." Geri Branton believes that the marriage was effectively over. All who talk about the trouble between Nat
and Maria mention Las Vegas.

Kelly was too young at the time to understand what was going on, but
he says, "When I think of the few times I heard them arguing, I think of
Vegas. There was always some sort of conflict. There were all the
temptations there—gambling, for one. He was not a big gambler, but one
time he went down to the casino with Sammy Davis, Jr., and they each
lost ten thousand dollars, or so the story goes. And that is what Mom

would not let happen to her husband. It could have happened to him, because money meant nothing to him when he had that kind of earning power. With a voice like that and a smile like that in your soul, what do you need to think about money for?"

Apparently, gambling was not the only Las Vegas temptation to which Nat Cole responded. Another was women. There were groupies in every city, of course. "You listen to his music, the type of sensuality it conveyed, the type of audience response it evoked, and groupies were inevitable," says Kelly. But there was a sense of abandon in Las Vegas that made the groupies there especially deadly; and given those circumstances one might have expected Maria to have insisted on accompanying Nat there. But she did not; she had stopped going to Vegas. "She wouldn't come to Vegas," says Carl Carruthers. "She despised it." Lots of people knew how those white girls felt about Nat up there, and she couldn't control it."

Carruthers had left Cole's employ in 1958, after nine years, and subsequently toured with Count Basie, Sarah Vaughan, Sammy Davis, Jr., Duke Ellington, and the Platters. In 1964 he rejoined Cole. "He had this big road show—thirty or forty people, different big artists—and he wasn't covered the way I used to cover him, taking care of the sound and the transportation and all that. I was living in New York, and when he played at the Copa I went to see him. He wanted me to go back with him, and I did, changed a lot of things around." Carruthers remembers that Cole did a lot of "hanging out" in Vegas: "That's where we had our fun."

"He had a lot of girl friends," says Geri Branton. "They loved him in Vegas. And he'd come home, and you'd see his face just drop, because there he was in this beautiful home with all the trappings, and he couldn't be comfortable in his own home. . . . He would hate to leave Vegas. He would extend his stay in Vegas to *keep* from going home."

One young woman whose name has been linked with Cole's was a singer and dancer in the *Sights and Sounds* show. Some believe that Maria may have known about her.

Carol Cole was old enough to understand that there was trouble between her parents, but she had her own problems. She graduated from Cazenovia Junior College in upstate New York that spring of 1964. "My father came to my graduation. My mother, for reasons I don't fully understand, was very angry with me, so she didn't come. Then I went off to do summer stock with John Kenley's semiprofessional company. We worked at two theaters, one in Warren, Ohio, and one in Columbus, and while I was out there I received some letters from my mother that suggested that things weren't so wonderful at home." But Carol was too stagestruck to take the matter seriously. Besides, she couldn't imagine her parents not being together. In the late summer she went to New York, where her father visited her once, but he didn't choose to burden her with his problems.

That late summer and early fall of 1964, Cole was carrying a heavier schedule than usual. He was appearing with *Sights and Sounds* in Lake Tahoe and at the same time filming *Cat Ballou* (which starred Lee Marvin), in which he and Stubby Kaye played a sort of interracial Greek chorus. Dressed in Western garb and plucking banjos, they sang "The Ballad of Cat Ballou" and provided a running musical commentary on the action in the film. Wrote Pauline Kael in her review of the film, "There are even two minstrels. Wasn't Cole enough? Is it perhaps that Stubby Kaye makes it cuter? A black man and a fat man—so nobody can fail to realize that the ballad singing is 'for fun.'" Cole was aware that he was being exploited, but he planned to record the title song from the film and to exploit the popularity of the film to sell records.

He would finish his last show at Harrah's in Lake Tahoe, then catch a plane for Hollywood. Late in the afternoon, after working in *Cat Ballou*, he would fly back to Tahoe for the evening show. He got little sleep and looked and felt exhausted. He also began to lose weight, which worried the people around him, for he was very slim as it was. But everyone blamed his heavy schedule and expected that he would feel better once he completed filming *Cat Ballou*.

From Harrah's in Lake Tahoe, the show moved on to the Sands in Las Vegas. Carl Carruthers recalls that when in Las Vegas Nat always went out after the last show and so he was surprised the first night at the Sands when Nat went directly to his hotel suite after the show. "He said, 'Carl, I have a pain. I can't walk.' I wanted to take him to the hospital, but he said, 'I'm not going to the hospital, Carl. It's bad publicity.' So we had a doctor come with a portable EKG [electrocardiogram] unit. The doctor said he should rest a few days, and we didn't think too much more about it." Cole informed his people that he didn't want Maria to know what had happened.

Carruthers remembers, "Then we went to the San Carlos in San Francisco, and it happened again. I had to revamp the show on the spot, put him on first and get him out of there." Cole was staying at the Fairmont Hotel, and one of the hotel physicians suggested he have a chest X ray. Wrote Maria in her book, "'From the minute we looked at the X rays,' the doctor was to tell me later, 'we were all broken up. It was obvious that he only had a couple of months.'" Cole had a large tumor on his left lung.

He began to take antibiotics, but he didn't heed the advice of doctors to cancel his engagements. Not until early December did he give in and allow himself to be admitted to Saint John's Hospital in Santa Monica. And not until then was Maria informed of her husband's illness.

She'd been spending most of her time in New York, where they kept an apartment, and had just returned from ten days in Europe when her sister Charlotte called to tell her to return home. By the time she arrived in Los Angeles, Nat had entered the hospital.

Cole didn't want the press to know that he had been hospitalized, and for the first week or so they managed to keep his illness a secret. The reason for his cancellation of a concert on December 11 to dedicate Los Angeles's new music center was given simply as "illness." Frank Sinatra filled in for him. But when Cole's doctors decided to try cobalt treatments, it was impossible to keep the secret: Cole had to go to a laboratory outside the hospital for the treatments.

The story broke on December 16. That's how Carol Cole learned about her father's illness. In New York "I was preparing to return to L.A. for the holidays, and I heard over the radio that my father was in the hospital. It was just bizarre. I thought there must be some mistake because I had not received any communication from my family that my father was even sick. I spoke to Charlotte, and she said that the news release had gone out without the permission of my mother. She said yes, I should come home."

Actually, the news release had not said Cole was dying. In fact, it painted a far more optimistic picture than the real situation. Drs. Robert

Kositchek and Elmer Rigby reported, "After exhaustive X rays and other tests, it has been discovered that Mr. Cole has a lung tumor. We anticipate that he will be released in approximately ten days, when he will return to his home. We had advised Mr. Cole that his professional engagements for the next few months must be canceled."

The reason Cole was to be allowed to go home in less than two weeks was that it would be Christmas, and his doctors were quite sure that it would be his last. Carol understood this as soon as she reached L.A. The cancer was anaplastic and spreading hourly.

The story of Cole's illness was carried in newspapers and on radio; Ed Sullivan announced that Cole was in the hospital on his weekly television show. "After that there was, literally, a deluge of mail, from all over the world. It was quite astounding," says Carol. "My mother gave me the task of going through the mail, answering some of the letters, putting some aside to be kept, making lists of the people who were known, to some extent, to be acknowledged. Some of the letters were from people who begged my mother to take Dad out of the country to Mexico, Sweden for treatment. No one was saying there was a sure cure for cancer, but they were saying that these alternative treatments might be more helpful than what was going on."

Geri Branton recalls that Doris Duke was among those who tried to persuade Maria to try another approach. "She sent for Maria, and a friend and I went with her. She lived in a house that had belonged to Valentino, Fox's Lair, a house like an old museum—huge living room, worn furniture, six wolfhounds. She wanted to send Nat to Duke University Hospital because there was a doctor there who was trying different methods. He wanted to remove the left lung." But he never went.

"The marriage was practically over," Geri Branton feels. "Leo and his friends really worked at keeping it together. So I would have to surmise ... that his illness really saved [the marriage]."

Carl Carruthers agrees. He never saw Cole again after he entered the hospital, although he did speak to him by telephone. Many of Cole's friends say they were unable to contact him at that time. "After Nat's death, I told Marie, 'You're the luckiest woman of the year. He would have put you out.'" But that, of course, is opinion.

Cole never had to make the decision whether or not to leave Maria.

Had he lived to do so, one wonders if he would have been able to leave her, despite what many saw as his unhappiness. Cole was a man who, over the course of his life, had put family and especially children at a premium. He had a son who was not yet six years old and twin daughters who were only three. Could he have subjected them to the bitterness of a divorce? He'd spent nearly twenty years trying to please Maria. Geri Branton suggests that perhaps because of his background, he had a deep-seated guilt that caused him to need to please. Could he have left the woman whose acceptance had been so important to him for so long?

For her part, Maria understood that her husband was dying. She had devoted seventeen years of her life to the man and his career. She was in her early forties, and she faced being completely alone. She'd come as far in her life as she had by being realistic, and she now took the steps that were necessary to ensure that she lost nothing more.

Maria wrote in her book that she was at the hospital every day; she was also making changes in her and her husband's legal affairs, as well as in their social relationships. To many of those around her, it seemed that she demanded that people choose sides—either they were on her side or they were on his. It pained these people to do so. Sparky was fired, as was Carl Carruthers. "I think it is a sadness," says Carol Cole. "To my knowledge, a good handful of people were cut off, and in my opinion they were the gems, the ones who were real and who loved unconditionally. I'm sure my mother had multiple reasons, but she just . . . canceled."

Cole signed a new will around this time; when he did so he was very ill.

His rapidly worsening condition made it impossible for him to go home for Christmas. Instead, the entire family gathered at his bedside. Of the children only Carol and Natalie were old enough to understand what was happening. Cole was able to go home for two days at New Year's but had to be attended by nurses around the clock. When he saw the piles of mail that had come for him, he brightened, Maria says, and asked, "Is all that for me?" Maria wrote that after Christmas they became very close, "like in the days when we first met." By the third week of January, his doctors were forced to conclude that the cobalt treatments were having no effect, and on January 25 they removed his left lung.

Cole's father, meanwhile, was seriously ill in Chicago, and the news of his son's grave illness was kept from him. Cole called his father several times from the hospital, pretending that he was calling from home and with all the cheerfulness he could muster. The Reverend Mr. Coles died five days after Cole's lung was removed. Cole's doctors and family considered not telling him, then realized he would see it on television or read it in the newspapers. When they told him, he showed no visible reaction, but his brother Eddie believed that the news accounted for his subsequent turn for the worse.

Cole lingered on for two more weeks, saying little, too weak to speak or even raise his head. Apparently he never discussed his impending death, even with his wife, and there is no way to know the extent of his private torment. While he was still lucid, he talked about how important it was to warn children against smoking and expressed interest in doing advertisements for the American Cancer Society, but he was soon too weak and wracked with pain to do so. Toward the end he was so heavily sedated that he was probably unable to think clearly. One hopes that he was relatively free of pain and of terror. As long as he was able, he visited the hospital chapel daily, and no doubt he found comfort in his religion at that time.

He died on February 15, 1965, a month and two days before his forty-sixth birthday.

The world mourned the passing of Nat King Cole; his death had come as something of a shock to the public, for all press releases had been written and issued by Maria and had been optimistic in tone. Obituary writers spoke of his "exemplary life." An editorial in the *Birmingham* (Alabama) *News* described him as an entertainer of "good taste and dignity." At the funeral four days after his death, four hundred people, the majority of them in the entertainment business, crowded into Saint James Episcopal Church to hear Jack Benny eulogize Cole as a man "who gave so much and still had so much more to give." Benny had been the last show business figure to visit Cole before his death. "Sometimes death isn't as tragic as not knowing how to live," said Benny. "This nice man knew how to live—and knew how to make others glad they were living." Another fifteen hundred people stood outside the church, among them Irving Ashby and the woman whose name had been linked to Cole's in Las Vegas. All five children attended the funeral and accompanied the casket to the Freedom Mausoleum at Forest Lawn Memorial Park in

Glendale. There, Cole was laid to rest in a crypt adjoining those of comedian Gracie Allen and actor Alan Ladd.

Cole's will was filed for probate in Los Angeles on February 26. Except for small bequests to relatives, he left everything to Maria and the children. There was no estimate of the estate's worth, but according to Geri Branton it was sizeable. Most of it went to Maria. By the terms of the new will that Cole had signed while in the hospital, small provisions were made for the children's education but that was all. "We're talking about thirty thousand to forty thousand, which he could make in one good weekend in Vegas," says Kelly. "Considering the bulk of the estate, it was very little."

11

The
Legacy

B EFORE Cole had been stricken with lung cancer, he had planned to produce James Baldwin's play *Amen Corner,* and Maria went ahead with those plans. The play opened in New York on April 15, two months after Cole's death; and Maria attended the premiere with Baldwin. She had put up seventy-five percent of the financing.

She had become a businesswoman "whether she wanted to or not," she explained to reporters, and indeed, Cole's estate was large and complicated. In his lifetime he had made more than six hundred recordings and made investments in a variety of areas. His estate was being administered by one attorney, one business manager, and two trustees, and so she was not responsible for it on a daily basis; but initially she was most interested in how it was handled, just as she had been interested in her husband's business affairs when he was alive.

For many months after Cole's death, Maria devoted herself to his

171

affairs and his memory. On the day of his funeral, she announced the formation of the Nat King Cole Cancer Foundation, and she devoted much of her time to that cause. The foundation didn't exist very long, however. Geri Branton believes it was because Maria aimed too high in asking people to help her with it. "She asked impossible people, people who had their own agendas and who had better things to do than help her." Eventually Maria decided to take the fifty thousand dollars she had raised and to donate a room in the Wilson Pavilion of the UCLA Medical Center. She wrote in her book that she was miffed when the chancellor of the university barely acknowledged her at the dedication ceremony.

In late 1966 Maria tried again at resuming her singing career. She debuted in Australia and then returned to the United States, hoping to get enough bookings in small clubs to perfect her act and gain entree to larger clubs. Among those who helped her were Ed Sullivan and Duke Ellington. In late January 1967 she appeared on the "Ed Sullivan Show" with the Duke. "Maria, who's a very talented torch singer, sang with Duke for two years before her marriage to Nat," Sullivan told reporters. "I thought it might make her feel at home to work with him on our show." She found, however, that there weren't enough small clubs that met her standards; as she explained in the epilogue of her book, after a few engagements she decided to quit "rather than appear in places that would have, in the public's eye, diminished the image of Mrs. Nat Cole." For a time she cohosted a show on the local Los Angeles station KHJ-TV, interviewing a variety of prominent people, black and white.

In the late 1960s Louie Robinson, who had interviewed her and Nat for *Ebony,* assisted her in writing *Nat King Cole: An Intimate Biography.* Published by William Morrow & Company in 1971, it was a thin volume that revealed more about Maria Cole than it did about her husband. One reviewer found it lacking in insight and psychological depth, and another chided that it provided only glimpses into his life; acquaintances considered it a compilation of "fantasies" and evidence of Maria's not having recognized her husband's feelings about their relationship. As an example, she quoted her husband as having once said, "If I am ever reincarnated, I want to come back as my wife—nobody else ever had it so good." Intimates of the family profess to see irony in that statement.

Nellie Lutcher says that what Maria wrote about her is simply not true.

"Young people reading that book would think I was a lousy entertainer," she explains. Lutcher is concerned, now, as she has been since the book came out, only with setting the record straight.

Having completed her book, Maria donated her late husband's gold records, various other awards, the scrapbooks her sister, Charlotte Sullivan, had kept over the years, and assorted photographs and correspondence to the Doheney Library at the University of Southern California. Her children go there to learn about their father's career.

Maria kept busy with charity and cultural work of one sort or another. Otherwise, she did not socialize much.

Around 1971 she remarried. Her new husband, Gary Devore, was a white screenwriter twenty years her junior. There were difficulties from the start. For Devore, it was hard to adjust to having a readymade family, especially when Carol was only two years younger than he. It was also difficult living in Los Angeles in the shadow of Nat King Cole. Deciding they would have to leave eventually, they purchased a house in Tyringham, Massachusetts, and began spending summers and Christmases there, then moved East permanently around 1973. They were divorced around 1976.

Maria has kept the house and divides her time between there and a condominium at the Ritz Hotel in Boston. There in 1981 she hosted a radio show for a time. She serves on the board of the Boston Symphony and otherwise keeps busy. She has no money worries. "She has a tremendous income," says Geri Branton. "Leo fixed it so that . . . she's paid by the year." Maria has not remarried.

"She has held her age very well," says Kelly. "She's a beautiful woman. I remember when Lena Horne was doing *Pal Joey* in L.A. around 1978. We went to see it and then went backstage. Together those two women added up to about one hundred seventeen years old, and they were the two most attractive women in the place." Maria takes seriously her position as Nat King Cole's widow and guards his legacy carefully.

She is not close to her children. "It's a decision that she made a long, long time ago," says Kelly. "I don't know if it was right or wrong. What's wrong about it was that he died—he's not around anymore and *we* are—and she kind of sacrificed her closeness with her kids for her closeness with her husband, who did not live to reap the benefits of that closeness. It would be great if he were alive and sixty-five now and they were close and they had one another, no matter what the relationship with the kids. Unfortunately, he did not live."

Carol Cole remained in Los Angeles after her father's death. "I managed to get a screen test at Columbia. They had a contract-player program and I got into that. Harrison Ford came out of that program; Terry Garr was in it; I was the only black, needless to say. I had a couple of parts, including a part in one of the Matt Helm films with Dean Martin, which was fluff, stupid. They really didn't know what to do with me; they knew that I had talent, but they didn't have much to offer.

"The theater was closest to my heart. I did the first West Coast production of *The Owl and the Pussycat,* which Diana Sands had done on Broadway. That kind of made the studio wake up. But it was clear that they weren't going to be very helpful, and I left Columbia and went to New York. I made my little Broadway debut in a Gore Vidal play, *Weekend,* a political comedy that was about two weeks on the boards."

After that, Carol returned to Hollywood and made another film for Columbia—*The Mad Room* with Stella Stevens and Shelley Winters. "It was a stupid movie," says Carol, "but since my role as a secretary was not written black, they thought they had done a *wonderful thing* by giving it to me." Conditions for blacks in Hollywood hadn't changed much since the time Nat King Cole had tried to break into films.

Television had begun to open up for blacks. Around that time Carol was offered a role in the show *Julia,* which starred Diahann Carroll, and which from the first was denigrated by militant blacks as being an "Aunt Jemima" kind of show. Carol turned it down. "I had certain political feelings at that time," she explains, "and I am sure I was still mourning in my own way. My mother has never forgiven me for turning that down."

Currently, Carol is associate producer of *Tar Baby,* the film version of the award-winning novel by Toni Morrison. She lives with her husband and children and is working on a book about her father. "There's this overwhelming sense of goodness," she says, referring to the information she has found. "He was a kind and gentle man." In the course of doing that book, she no doubt hopes to learn more about herself.

Natalie Cole seems to have been destined for a career in entertainment;

by the age of five she'd been on Art Linkletter's TV show "Kids Say the Darndest Things" twice. She made her first stage appearance at age eleven singing "It's a Bore" in her father's production of *I'm with You* at the Greek Theater in Los Angeles. While attending Catholic high school, Natalie decided for a time that she was going to be a doctor, but her father's death when she was fifteen seems to have cemented the resolve of the child who looked most like Nat King Cole to carry on his name in show business.

At the University of Massachusetts in Amherst she met Taj Mahal, who impressed her with his ability to assimilate various black folk styles. After graduating from U Mass, she stayed on in Amherst, taking a job as a waitress in a local club called the Pub. While there she joined a local band that performed in the area on weekends. She made her first professional appearance on July 4, 1971, and her club engagements increased steadily after that. In 1973 she made her first lengthy club tour, starting at the Copacabana.

In October 1974, while appearing at Mr. Kelly's in Chicago, she met Chuck Jackson and Marvin Yancy. They took her to Curtis Mayfield's Curtom Studios, where they wrote and produced an entire album for her. They offered the finished product, *Inseparable,* to Capitol Records, her father's old label, and Capitol immediately signed her to a contract. "Daddy would have been pleased," she said. "I think my being on Capitol would have knocked him out."

The album, which was released in 1975, went straight to the top of the R & B charts and produced two hit singles, the title track and "This Will Be." At the 1976 Grammy Awards, Natalie took the prizes for both New Artist of the Year and Best R & B Female Vocal Performance for "This Will Be." That same year she and Marvin Yancy were secretly married, and two years later their son, Robbie, was born.

Over the next few years, Natalie recorded six more albums for Capitol and picked up a third Grammy. She also became addicted to drugs, developed polyps on her throat that caused her to lose her voice, and got divorced. Around 1981 she made a serious effort to overcome the variety of emotional and chemical demons that were destroying her. She turned over to her mother control of her affairs in a court-sanctioned conservatorship and entered a rehabilitation program. After that she had surgery to remove the polyps on her throat. She hired a new manager, restructured her financial affairs, and started work on a new album. Her ex-husband, Marvin Yancy, produced *I'm Really*; it was their first collaboration in three years. She thought she could handle it and her first concert tour in nearly that long. But she could not. In late 1983 she was back at the rehabilitation center, determined this time to battle her problems and win.

Natalie Cole has had many demons. Some may have taken up residence inside her shortly after she was born—she came to feel that she was not altogether welcomed by her mother; she'd been expected to be a boy by her father, remained unnamed for several days, and was rather too dark-complexioned for bourgeois black tastes. She suffered as much as the other children from not having her parents around much when she was growing up. Natalie paid dearly for having a sensitivity and a loving nature that caused her to reach out to her father's side of the family: She suffered for all the wrongs, real and imagined, that the Coles of Chicago had endured since Nat had married Maria.

"She was trying to right a wrong," says Kelly. "All our lives we had been kept from half of our family, and when Natalie started to do well, she said to herself, 'What is half of me about? I want to find out who these people are.' So she went to see them . . . I feel that's what messed things up. [One of them] was Natalie's 'spiritual adviser,' and we know where Natalie is now."

Kelly Cole had turned six about a week before his father died. He was just old enough to have some inkling of the nature of death, and in her book Maria questions whether she was right to take him to the funeral and then to the cemetery. Family friends were also concerned that of all the children, Kelly might be most affected by his father's death. One, Edward G. Robinson, took it upon himself to become a surrogate father to Kelly.

"It wasn't every day or anything, maybe three times a month," says Kelly. "He would take me over to his house and show me his incredible art collection, explaining each piece to me and who the artist was. What I remember best was the Renoir—women bathing—because they were so fat and because it was probably the first time I'd seen a painting of nude women.

"He liked my painting. I used to paint things for him, and he was very enthusiastic and wanted to inspire me. We were very close up until he died in 1973. I was about fourteen. He was a good man—sweet and very gentle. In fact, when he played a gangster in *Little Caesar* they had to tape his eyes open, because every time he had to fire a revolver he would shut his eyes tight. Some tough guy!"

A few other friends of the family took a special interest in Kelly—Bing Crosby and Jack Benny among them—but they generally came only to escort his mother to some social function. Feeling that her son needed to be around a strong male role model, Maria sent Kelly to a ranch in Gillette, Wyoming, for three summers in a row. He wore cowboy clothes and learned to ride and hunt; he loved it.

Kelly had started school at UCLA's experimental University Elementary School, but after his father died—and perhaps after the chancellor of the university failed to acknowledge Maria Cole in a manner she regarded as fitting when she paid for a room at UCLA Medical Center— Kelly transferred to Buckley, a much more conservative private school. Kelly didn't do well there and required tutoring during the summer. "They thought I was dyslexic," he says, "but I was just a lazy reader. I went back East to Massachusetts the summer between sixth and seventh grade, and in just a couple of months I went from a third-grade reading level to reading all of Hemingway."

Spending summers in Massachusetts was one thing. Moving there when he was fourteen was quite another. "I was just getting into being an adolescent in Southern California and beginning to establish connections. I'd always been interested in film and at fourteen was very much into silent films. I wanted to write and eventually direct. I thought they [his mother and stepfather] were sick and crazy for moving there."

Kelly didn't attend school in Massachusetts but instead went away to boarding school—Kent School in Kent, Connecticut. It was his decision to go away. "That town [in Massachusetts] had about two hundred and fifty people," he says, "and there was nothing to do but have arguments with your parents." During his senior year at Kent, his mother and Gary Devore divorced.

After graduating from Kent, Kelly decided to return to California. "Natalie was doing very well, and I figured if I was going to make my mark in the entertainment business, I should get my act out there." He attended the "small, conservative" Rutland College, graduating with a major in literature and a minor in theater.

Kelly worked for a film production company, sold cars, sold books, and turned again to the entertainment field. He, too, is interested in writing about his father's life and is intrigued with the dimensions of his father that his research has unearthed. Once, going through his father's belongings that are still in the attic of the Massachusetts house, he came across a Marlene Dietrich album inscribed by Dietrich, "To Nat, without you this would not have been possible—Marlene." Says Kelly, "It's amazing. I just literally stumbled across this album going through the attic at South House. I didn't know that she had touched anybody's life in my family or how close they were. I would like to find out more about it."

The twins, Casey and Timolin, attended Buckley School, as Kelly had, then, after the family moved to Massachusetts, went to Northfield–Mount Herman, a private boarding school in Northfield, Massachusetts. Both took music lessons as children, but neither showed any strong interest in a musical career. At this writing, Casey is in Los Angeles and working for the U.S. Olympic Committee. Timolin is in college in Texas, majoring in broadcast journalism. They have only the vaguest recollection of their father.

Twenty years after his death, there were few people who had not heard of Nat King Cole. Anyone tuning in to an "easy listening" radio station was likely to hear one or more of a dozen or so songs that would always be associated with him—"Mona Lisa," "Too Young," "Nature Boy," "Lazy-Hazy-Crazy Days of Summer." With Cole, the association between artist and song is particularly close. As Henry Pleasants put it in his book, *The Great American Popular Singers,* "Nat Cole had a way of caressing a word, of wrapping his voice around it. So close, so intimate was this identification with the music implicit in language that I, for one, cannot evoke the memory of his voice without the words to go with it. One doesn't hear that voice simply as sound. One hears 'A blossom fell,' or 'Sweet Lorraine,' or 'Darling, Je vous aime beaucoup.'" Few people know, however, that he was one of the finest jazz pianists who ever lived, despite the fact that any number of jazz musicians mention his name when asked about their own early influences. Jazz aficionados do try to keep that memory alive: In the early 1980s, Billy Taylor did a show on the history of jazz for the Public Broadcasting System and Cole's name was mentioned frequently; and Bobby Scott performed a Living Tribute to Cole at the Village West in New York City in 1983.

The general public, however, does not know much about Cole. Actually they didn't know much about him while he was alive, for Cole was a very private person who rarely shared his private feelings. Except for Maria's book, there have been no biographies of Cole. Whether this is because he was black or because a number of people who knew and loved him have felt that they must remain silent is a moot question.

At this writing, ABC-TV plans to air a movie about his life, starring Dorian Harewood, known best to TV viewers for his appearances in *Roots II, The Buffalo Rangers,* and *The Jesse Owens Story.* Harewood, who is a singer, wanted to do his own vocalizing; but Maria insisted that he lip-sync her husband's songs, and at this writing, the producers of the TV movie had agreed to let her have the final word.

One wonders what Cole himself would have to say if he could speak to us. He probably would not wish to get involved in any controversy. He probably would like to be remembered as a consummate jazz artist and as one of the first blacks to make the vaunted crossover and appeal to white audiences. No doubt he would like to feel vindicated in his quiet, dignified, very nonradical manner of dealing with the "race problem" in America. But most of all, he probably would like to be remembered as a nice man, a man whose priority was taking care of his wife and children and making them happy whatever the cost to his own health or even happiness. He need not worry about that. Through his records and the way he sang his songs, he assured this legacy.

Discography

T HIS discography is a compilation from a variety of sources. No complete listing of Nat King Cole's singles issued and albums issued exists. Maria Cole's book includes recording dates and songs for Capitol. Capitol Records has lists of singles since June 1951 and albums since September 1949 (the company's earlier documents on Cole's recordings have been destroyed). Various jazz directories were consulted for recordings before Cole signed with Capitol and for the purpose of matching A and B sides of singles. This listing is primarily of U.S. releases only. Album or single disc number is included wherever possible, as is year of release.

Abbreviations

as	alto sax		p	piano
bs	bass		s	sax
dr	drum		t	trumpet
g	guitar		ts	tenor sax
			vcl	vocal

SINGLES

1936
With Eddie Cole's Solid Swingers (Kenneth Roane-t/Tommy Thompson-as, ts/Bill Wright-ts/Nat Cole-p/Eddie Cole-bs/Jimmy Adams-vcl)

Honey Hush/Thunder	Decca 7210
Stomping at the Panama/Bedtime	Decca 7215

1939
King Cole's Swingsters (Nat King Cole-p, vcl/Oscar Moore-g/Wesley Prince-bs/Bonnie Lake-vcl) (unable to match A and B sides except in one case)

Anesthetic for Lovers	Davis & Schwegler
Land of Make-Believe	Davis & Schwegler
Ta-De-Ah	Davis & Schwegler
Riffin' at the Bar-B-Q	Davis & Schwegler
I Lost Control of Myself/Let's Get Happy	Davis & Schwegler
That "Please Be Mineable" Feeling	Davis & Schwegler

King Cole Trio (as above, without Bonnie Lake) with Lionel Hampton Orchestra

Central Avenue Breakdown/Jack the Bellboy	Victor 26652
A Ghost of a Chance/Dough Re Mi	Victor 26696
Blue Because of You/Jivin' with Jarvis	Victor 26724
House of Morgan/I'd Be Lost without You	Victor 26751

1940
King Cole Trio (as above)

Sweet Lorraine/This Side Up	Decca 8520
Honeysuckle Rose/Gone with the Draft	Decca 8535

1941
King Cole Trio

Babs/Early Morning Blues	Decca 8541

Scotchin' with the Soda/Slow Down	Decca 8556
Hit the Ramp/This'll Make You Laugh	Decca 8571
Stop, the Red Light's On/I Like to Riff	Decca 8592
Call the Police/Are You Fer It?	Decca 8604
That Ain't Right/Hit That Jive, Jack	Decca 8630

King Cole Quartet (Cole-p, vcl/Lee Young-dr/unknown g&bs)

I Like to Riff/On the Sunny Side of the Street	Varsity 8340; Savoy 600; Ammor 108
Black Spider/By the River Sainte Marie	Ammor 109

1942
King Cole Quintet (Cole-p, vcl/Shad Collins-tpt/Illinois Jacquet-ts/ Gene Englund-bs/J.C. Heard-dr)

Heads/It Had to Be You	Disc 2010
I Can't Give You Anything but Love/Pro-sky	Disc 2011

King Cole Trio (Cole-p, vcl/Oscar Moore-g/Red Callender-bs)

Vom Vim Veedle/All for You	Excelsior 8114; Cap 139

1943
King Cole Trio (Cole-p, vcl/Oscar Moore-g/Johnny Miller-bs)

I'm Lost/Pitchin' Up a Boogie	Excelsior 105
Beautiful Moons Ago/Let's Spring One	Excelsior 107
F.S.T./My Lips Remember Your Kisses	Premier 100; Atlas 100
Let's Pretend/Got a Penny	Premier 103; Atlas 106

1943-1944*
King Cole Trio (as above)

Straighten Up and Fly Right/I Can't See for Lookin'	Capitol 154
Gee Baby, Ain't I Good to You/I realize Now	Capitol 169; V-Disc 339
If You Can't Smile and Say Yes/Bring Another Drink	Capitol 192

---

* four recording sessions between November 1943 and March 1944; most singles issued in 1944

I'm a Shy Guy/I Tho't You Ought to Know	Capitol 208
Come to Baby Do/The Frim Fram Sauce	Capitol 224
Route 66/Everyone Is Sayin' Hello Again	Capitol 256
Sweet Lorraine/Embraceable You	Capitol 20009
The Man I Love/Body and Soul	Capitol 20010
Prelude in C Sharp Minor/What Is This Thing Called Love	Capitol 20011
It's Only a Paper Moon/Easy Listenin' Blues	Capitol 20012
Jumpin' at Capitol	Capitol 10038

1945
King Cole Trio

If You Can't Smile . . ./A Pile of Cole	V-Disc 437
Any Old Time/Bring Another Drink	V-Disc 455
Candy/Trio Grooves in Brooklyn	V-Disc 499
Satchel Mouth Baby/Solid Potato Salad	V-Disc 508

1945-1946
King Cole Trio

What Can I Say After I Say I'm Sorry/This Way Out	Capitol 20061
I Know That You Know/I Don't Know Why	Capitol 20062
I'm in the Mood for Love/To a Wild Rose	Capitol 20063
Look What You've Done to Me/I'm Through with Love	Capitol 20064
Rex Rhumba/Kee-Mo Ky-Mo	Capitol 15240
Oh But I Do/You Call It Madness	Capitol 274
The Best Man/For Sentimental Reasons	Capitol 304
The Christmas Song [violin added]/In the Cool of the Evening	Capitol 311
But She's My Buddy's Chick/That's the Beginning of the End	Capitol 328
You Should Have Told Me/I Want to Thank Your Folks	Capitol 356
You Don't Learn That in School/Meet Me at No Special Place	Capitol 393
You're the Cream in My Coffee	Capitol 10086

1946

Nat King Cole (p, vcl), Joe Stafford (vcl) and orchestra accomp.

Candy	Capitol 259

1947

King Cole Trio (Johnny Mercer-vcl on V15000 and 15026)

Come in Out of the Rain/Can You Look Me in the Eyes	Capitol 418
Naughty Angeline/That's What	Capitol 437
I Miss You So/I Think I Get What You Mean	Capitol 444
Makin' Whoopee/Too Marvelous for Words	Capitol 10101
Honeysuckle Rose/I'll String Along with You	Capitol 10102
Rumba Azul/This Is My Night to Dream	Capitol 10103
If I Had You/When I Take My Sugar to Tea	Capitol 813
Save the Bones for Henry Jones/Harmony	Capitol 15000
Now He Tells Me/Those Things Money Can't Buy	Capitol 15011
What'll I Do?/I Feel So Smoochie	Capitol 15019
My Baby Likes to Bebop/You Can't Make Money Dreamin'	Capitol 15026
I've Only Myself to Blame/The Geek	Capitol 15036
Baby, Baby All the Time/Little Girl	Capitol 15165
Don't Blame Me/I've Got a Way With Women	Capitol 15010 or 15110
A Boy From Texas, a Girl from Tennessee/My Fair Lady	Capitol 15085
Flo and Joe/That's a Natural Fact	Capitol 15320
Smoke Gets in Your Eyes	Capitol 10074
Could Ja?	Capitol 20128
Laguna Mood	Capitol 15201

King Cole Trio (Irving Ashby replacing Oscar Moore on g)

Put 'em in a Box/It's the Sentimental Thing	Capitol 15080
Lillette/A Woman Always Understands	Capitol 15224
Portrait of Jennie [with orchestra]/An Old Piano Plays the Blues	Capitol 15387

If You Stub Your Toe on the Moon/Don't Cry, Cry Baby	Capitol 15418
Baby, Won't You Please Come Home	Capitol 15171

Nat King Cole (p, with rhythm)

Cole Capers/These Foolish Things	Capitol 10189
Three Little Words/I'll Never Be the Same	Capitol 10190
How High the Moon/Blues in My Shower	Capitol 10191

1948
Nat King Cole (vcl)

Nature Boy [acc. by Frank de Vol's Orch.]/ Lost April [acc. by Carlyle Hall Orch.]	Capitol 15054

1949
King Cole and Trio (Joe Comfort replacing Johnny Miller on bs; Jack Costanzo on bongo)

Lillian/Lush Life [acc. Pete Rugolo's Orch.]	Capitol 57-606
I Used to Love You/Bop-Kick	Capitol 57-641
Yes Sir, That's My Baby/'Tis Autumn	Capitol 57-642
For All We Know/Laugh! Cool Clown	Capitol 57-643
Who Do You Know in Heaven/The Trouble with You Is Me	Capitol 57-680
I Get Sentimental Over Nothing/Your Voice Land of Love [acc. Pete Rugolo's Orch.]	Capitol 57-716
You Can't Lose a Broken Heart [Starlighters, vcl]/ Nalani	Capitol 57-749
My Two Front Teeth [Starlighters, vcl]/	Capitol 57-90036
My Mother Told Me/Exactly Like You	Capitol 57-70050
Mule Train/My Baby Just Cares for Me [on both sides, Woody Herman-vcl with Cole, Gene Orloff-p]	Capitol 57-787
It Was So Good While It Lasted [acc. Pete Rugolo's Orch.]/ Bang Bang Boogie [Starlighters, vcl]	Capitol 818
The Horse Told Me/Don't Shove, I'm Leaving	Capitol 852
Baby, Won't You Say You Love Me/I Almost Lost My Mind [on both sides, no Costanzo; Starlighters-vcl]	Capitol 889

A Little Bit Independent/I'll Never Say "Never Again"
  Again [same personnel as on 889]   Capitol 1068

1950
King Cole and Trio

  Calypso Blues/Twisted Stockings [possibly Lee
    Young on dr, no Costanzo]   Capitol 915

King Cole and Trio [Nellie Lutcher, other instrum.]

  For You, My Love/Can I Come In for a Second?   Capitol 847

King Cole with Stan Kenton and Orch.

  Orange Colored Sky [Trio acc.]/Jam-Bo   Capitol 1184

1951
Nat King Cole (vcl), various accompaniments

  Early American/My Brother   Capitol 1565
  Sweet Lorraine/Kee-Mo Ky-Mo   Capitol 1613
  Lost April/Calypso Blues   Capitol 1627
  Embraceable You/It's Only a Paper Moon   Capitol 1650
  Nature Boy/For All We Know   Capitol 1663
  Make Believe Land/I'll Always Remember You   Capitol 1747
  Unforgettable/My First and My Last Love   Capitol 1808
  I'm Hurtin'/Walkin'   Capitol 1863
  Here's to My Lady/Miss Me   Capitol 1893

1952

  Makin' Whoopee/This Is My Night to Dream   Capitol 1669
  Wine, Women and Song/A Weaver of Dreams   Capitol 1925
  You Will Never Grow Old/You Weren't There   Capitol 1968
  Easter Sunday Morning/Summer Is A-Comin' In   Capitol 1994
  What Does It Take/Somewhere Along the Way   Capitol 2069
  Walkin' My Baby Back Home/Funny   Capitol 2130
  I'm Never Satisfied/Because You're Mine   Capitol 2212

Faith Can Move Mountains/Ruby and the Pearl	Capitol 2230
How/Strange	Capitol 2309

Nat King Cole (p), John Collins (g), Charlie Harris (bs), Bunny Shawker (dr)

Penthouse Serenade/If I Should Lose You	Capitol 15868
Somebody Loves Me/Down by the Old Mill Stream	Capitol 15869
Polka Dots and Moonbeams/Laura	Capitol 15870

1953

Nat King Cole (vcl), various accompaniments

Pretend/Don't Let Your Eyes Go Shopping	Capitol 2346
Lush Life/I Miss You So	Capitol 1672
Mona Lisa/No Moon At All	Capitol 1673
Too Young/For Sentimental Reasons	Capitol 1674
Blue Gardenia/Can't I	Capitol 2389
I Am in Love/My Flaming Heart	Capitol 2459
Return to Paradise/Angel Eyes	Capitol 2498
A Fool Was I/If Love Is Good to Me	Capitol 2540
Lover, Come Back to Me/That's All	Capitol 2610
Little Boy That Santa Claus Forgot/Mrs. Santa Claus	Capitol 2616
Answer Me, My Love/Why	Capitol 2687

1954

Alone too Long/It Happens to Me	Capitol 2754
Make Her Mine/I Envy	Capitol 2803
Pretend/Unforgettable	Capitol 1689
Smile/It's Crazy	Capitol 2897
Open Up the Doghouse/Long Long Ago [with Dean Martin]	Capitol 2985

1955

(In the middle of this year, Cole disbanded Trio)

A Blossom Fell/If I May [with the Four Knights]   Capitol 3095
The Sand and the Sea/Darling, Je Vous Aime Beaucoup Capitol 3027
Toyland/I'm Gonna Laugh You Right Out of My LIfe   Capitol 3305
My One Sin/   Capitol 3136
Someone You Love/Forgive My Heart   Capitol 3234

1956

Ask Me/Nothing Ever Changes My Love for You   Capitol 3328
Too Young to Go Steady/Never Let Me Go   Capitol 3390
That's All There Is to That [with the Four Knights]/
    My Dream Sonata   Capitol 3456
Night Lights/To the Ends of the Earth   Capitol 3551
Mrs. Santa Claus/Take Me Back to Toyland   Capitol 3560
The Christmas Song/The Little Boy that Santa
    Claus Forgot   Capitol 3561

1957

You Are My First Love/Ballerina   Capitol 3619
When Rock and Roll Came to Trinidad/China Gate   Capitol 3702
Send for Me/My Personal Possession [with the
    Four Knights]   Capitol 3737
Raintree County/With You on My Mind   Capitol 3782
Angel Smile/Back in My Arms   Capitol 3862 or 3860

1958

Do I Like It/Looking Back   Capitol 3939
Come Closer to Me/Nothing in the World   Capitol 4004
Non Dimenticar/Bend a Little My Way   Capitol 4056

1959

Madrid, Give Me Your Love   Capitol 4125
You Made Me Love You/I Must Be Dreaming   Capitol 4184
The Sweet Bird of Youth/Midnight Flyer   Capitol 4248

The Happiest Christmas Tree/Buon Natale	Capitol 4301
Time and the River/Whatcha' Gonna Do	Capitol 4325

1960

Is It Better to Have Loved and Lost/That's You	Capitol 4369
My Love/Steady [with Stan Kenton]	Capitol 4393
If I Knew/The World in My Arms	Capitol 4481

1961

Illusion/When It's Over	Capitol 4519
Mona Lisa/Unforgettable	Capitol 4115
Goodnight, Little Leaguer/The First Baseball Game	Capitol 4555
Take a Fool's Advice/Make It Last	Capitol 4582
Cappuccina/Let True Love Begin	Capitol 4623
Magic Moment/Step Right Up	Capitol 4672

1962

Too Young/Mona Lisa	Capitol A-6003
Look No Further/The Right Thing to Say	Capitol 4714
Looking Back/Send for Me	Capitol A-6029
The Good Times/Ramblin' Rose	Capitol 4804
Dear Lonely Hearts/Who's Next in Line?	Capitol 4870

1963

All Over the World/Nothing Goes Up	Capitol 4919
Those Lazy-Hazy-Crazy Days of Summer/ In the Cool of the Day	Capitol 4965
That Sunday, That Summer/Mr. Wishing Well	Capitol 5027
Lush Life/Straighten Up and Fly Right	Capitol 6036
Unforgettable/Somewhere Along the Way	Capitol A-6044

1964

My True Carrie, Love/A Rag, a Bone and a Hank of Hair	Capitol 5125

People/I Don't Want to Be Hurt Anymore	Capitol 5155
Marnie/More and More of Your Amor	Capitol 5219
Those Lazy-Hazy-Crazy Days of Summer/	
Our Old Home Team	Capitol 6051
I Don't Want to See Tomorrow/Love	Capitol 5261

1965

The Ballad of Cat Ballou/They Can't Make Her Cry	Capitol 5412
Sweet Lorraine/Nature Boy	Capitol A-6068
Wanderlust/You'll See	Capitol 5486
Looking Back/One Sun	Capitol 5549

1966

Let Me Tell You, Babe/For the Want of a Kiss	Capitol 5683
The Good Times/Ramblin' Rose	Capitol A-6099

1968

Thank You, Pretty Baby/Brazilian Love Song	Capitol 2088

1969

People/I'm Gonna Laugh You Right Out of My Life	Capitol 2451

1972

Jet/Portrait of Jennie	Capitol A-6179

1974

Those Lazy-Hazy-Crazy Days of Summer/	
That Sunday, That Summer	Capitol A-6211

ALBUMS

1942

Philo & Aladdin Album I (12″)

1944

King Cole Trio, Vol. 1

1946?

King Cole Trio, Vol. II

1948

King Cole Trio, Vol. III
King Cole for Kids   DC-89

1949

King Cole Trio, Vol. IV   H-177

1950

Harvest of Hits   H-213
Nat King Cole at the Piano   H-156
King Cole Trio, Vol. 1   H-220

1952

Penthouse Serenade   DT-332
Cole's Top Pops   H-9110

1953

Nat King Cole Sings for Two in Love   DT-420

1955

Nat King Cole 10th Anniversary Album   W-514
Vocal Classics   T-591
Instrumental Classics   T-592

1956

Ballads of the Day   DT-680
Piano Style of Nat King Cole   DT-689

1957

After Midnight	W-782
Love Is the Thing	SW-824
This Is Nat King Cole	DT-870

1958

Just One of Those Things	SW-903
St. Louis Blues	W-993
Cole Español	DW-1031
The Very Thought of You	SW-1084

1959

Welcome to the Club	W-1120
To Whom It May Concern	SW-1190
A Mis Amigos	SW-1220
Everytime I Feel the Spirit	SW-1249

1960

Tell Me All About Yourself	SW-1331
Wild Is Love	SWAK-1392
Magic of Christmas	SW-1444

1961

Touch of Your Lips	SW-1574
Nat Cole Story	SWCL-1613

1962

Cole Sings, Shearing Plays	SW-1675
Swingin' Side of Cole	SW-1724
More Cole Español	SW-1749
Ramblin' Rose	ST-1793
Dear Lonely Hearts	ST-1838

1963

Where Did Everyone Go?	SW-1859
Top Pops	DT-1891
Those Lazy, Hazy Crazy Days	ST-1932

1964

Let's Face the Music	SW-2008
I Don't Want to Be Hurt Anymore	ST-2118
My Fair Lady	SW-2117

1965

L-O-V-E	ST-2195
Nat King Cole Trio	T-2311
Cole Sings His Songs from *Cat Ballou*	ST-2340
Looking Back	ST-2361
Unforgettable	DT-357

1966

Nat King Cole Sings Hymns and Spirituals	ST-2454
Cole at the Sands	SMAS-2434
Nature Boy	DT-2348
Vintage Years	T-2529
Unforgettable Nat King Cole Sings Great Songs	ST-2558

1967

Sincerely	ST-2680
Thank You, Pretty Baby	ST-2759
Beautiful Ballads	ST-2820

1968

Best of Nat Cole	ST-2944
Nat King Cole Deluxe Set	STCL-2873

1969

Smile	ST-2943
Close-Up	DWBB-252
There, I've Said It Again	ST-310
Nat Cole's Greatest	SKAO-373

1970

Dear Lonely Hearts	SY-4577 GRAB

1972

Capitol Jazz Classics, Vol. 8	M-11033

1974

Love Is Here to Stay	SWAK-11355

1978

After Midnight	SM-11796
Nat King Cole Sings His Songs From *Cat Ballou*	SM-11804

1979

Looking Back	SM-11882
A Mis Amigos	SN-11962

1980

St. Louis Blues	SN-12059
Rablin' Rose	SN-16032
The Nat King Cole Story, Vol. I	SN-16033
The Nat King Cole Story, Vol. II	SN-16034
The Nat King Cole Story, Vol. III	SN-16035
The Best of Nat King Cole	SN-16036
Wild Is Love	SN-16037
A Mis Amigos	SN-16137

1981

Unforgettable	SN-16162
Love Is the Thing	SN-16163
Walkin' My Baby Back Home	DN-16164
A Blossom Fell	DN-16165
Cole Español	N-16166
More Cole Español	SN-16167

1982

The Best of Nat Cole Trio, Vol. I	N-16260
The Best of Nat Cole Trio, Vol. II	N-16261

INDEX

197